YOUTH, FAMILY

AND CITIZENSHIP

YOUTH, FAMILY
AND CITIZENSHIP

GILL JONES AND CLAIRE WALLACE

Open University Press
Buckingham · Philadelphia

Open University Press
Celtic Court
22 Ballmoor
Buckingham
MK18 1XW

and
1900 Frost Road, Suite 101
Bristol, PA 19007, USA

First Published 1992

A catalogue record of this book is available from the
British Library

Library of Congress Cataloging-in-Publication Data

Jones, Gill, 1942–
    Youth, family, and citizenship / Gill Jones and Claire Wallace.
        p. cm.
    Includes bibliographical references (p. 160) and indexes.
    ISBN 0-335-09299-3 (hb) — ISBN 0-335-09294-2 (pb)
    1. Youth—Great Britain—Economic conditions.   2. Youth—Great
Britain—Family relationships.   3. Youth as consumers—Great
Britain.   I. Wallace. Claire.   II. Title.
HQ799.G766 1992
305.23'5'0941–dc20   91–45491
                                                              CIP

Typeset by Inforum, Rowlands Castle, Hants
Printed in Great Britain by St Edmundsbury Press
Bury St Edmunds, Suffolk

CONTENTS

LIST OF FIGURES

AND TABLES

PREFACE

This book has developed over many years of academic and personal friendship between us. It has always been apparent to us both that though our research methods were different – Claire being a mainly ethnographic researcher while Gill has been mainly involved in large-scale survey research – many of the research problems we were tackling were similar, as were many of the ways we were tackling them. For both of us, it has been important to take a longitudinal approach to researching young people's lives, and both of us have been concerned with the need for a 'holistic' approach to youth. It was therefore inevitable that we should pool our ideas. So despite the problems of communication when we have been geographically very distanced (Claire moving between Plymouth, Lancaster and Prague, and Gill between London and Edinburgh), we have managed through very occasional but very intensive discussion to develop our ideas further and to put them into book form. The focus changed during this period, from a study of young people's experiences of family life and state interventions, to a focus on citizenship, the concept which both enabled us to connect private life transitions with more general public processes, and helped us to clarify other concepts more frequently used in the sociology of youth: the concepts of dependency, adulthood and emancipation. This volume is the result.

We have both been involved in researching aspects of youth while writing this book. Gill has been working at the Centre for Educational Sociology, The University of Edinburgh. Her work on the Scottish Young People's Survey has included research on the transition to economic independence and household formation in youth and was funded at various stages by the Scottish Office Education Department, Scottish Homes, the Joseph Rowntree Foundation, and the Economic and Social Research Council. Meanwhile, Claire has been involved in a project on youth in rural areas of south-west England, as part of the ESRC 16–19 Initiative, and more recently has been undertaking a cross-national study of dependency and independence in life-transitions in Germany, Britain and Poland, funded by the Anglo-German Foundation and the ESRC. Currently, Claire is seconded from Lancaster University in order to set up a social policy course at the Central European University in Prague, while Gill is involved in a two-year project, funded by the Joseph Rowntree Foundation, researching young people's experiences of the housing market and of homelessness in Scotland.

We have been helped in the preparation of this book by many people. Ideas have been generated by colleagues in Edinburgh, Lancaster and Plymouth. In particular, we would wish to thank Janet Finch, David Raffe and Adrian Sinfield for being so generous with their time in reading an earlier draft of the manuscript and for their very helpful suggestions. Our thanks to all of those who have given us feedback and support in seminars and informal conversations. In this respect, we would wish to thank John and Gill Stewart, and Moira Peelo at the University of Lancaster, and members of the women's reading group at Edinburgh. Claire would like to thank members of her third year Research Methods class in Social Policy at Lancaster University (1990/91) for their help with some data collection. The final draft of the text was produced with the help of Carolyn Newton and was proof read by Joan Hughes. Our thanks to them both, and other members of the Centre for Educational Sociology for their help in the preparation of the manuscript.

The bulk of our thanks should, however, go to those without whose help it would have been very difficult indeed to write this book: the young people who have taken part in the various surveys and interviews which have produced most of our findings and ideas.

1

YOUTH, FAMILY

AND CITIZENSHIP

How often have you heard parents, talking of their adolescent children, say things like 'She lives her own life these days, I don't interfere', or heard government ministers make statements such as 'We want to give people the right to choose'? Comments such as these are the constant rhetoric of parents and politicians. They suggest that there is self-determination in youth. This book considers the relevance of such statements to the lives of young people in Britain.

In the following chapters we shall be exploring the ways in which the transition from dependent child to independent adult is shaped by relationships with family members, the market-place and the institutions of the state. We shall argue that as young people become adult, they are faced with contradictory pressures coming from these various sources, to behave in different ways. The contradictions are, in our view, mainly to do with the ways in which the ideology of dependence and independence conflicts with normative practices. The question that arises in the course of this book is how young people growing up come to be recognized as independent citizens (with the rights as well as the obligations of citizenship) and to what extent this recognition is determined by their economic circumstances and level of dependency.

At the same time, we examine the concept of self-determination in youth and consider how much freedom young people really have to make decisions which may affect the rest of their lives. Throughout the book we identify inequalities of opportunity and choice between young people – inequalities stemming from their social class, their gender, their race or ethnicity, their geographical location and their economic status.

ORGANIZATION OF THE BOOK

We start by examining in this chapter the ways in which young people and their relationships with their families of origin have been treated in sociological research. We consider how far the traditional 'modernist' ideas and recent ideas emanating from post-modernism and/or high modernity can be applied to young people, and we propose a theoretical framework, based on the concept of citizenship, which we believe provides a new aproach to understanding youth and adulthood, dependence and independence. Citizenship embodies more than any other concept the notion of the rights and obligations of adults in our society.

We move on to consider the transitions to adulthood within this framework. Throughout, we examine the ways in which the changing structures, of family composition, of the labour market, of the welfare state, and so on, affect individual movement and increase or limit the choices available. The next two chapters focus on the ways in which the transition to adulthood is structured by policy. Chapter 2 considers young people's changing transitions into work and the labour market and the ways in which these transitions have been structured by state intervention and market needs. Chapter 3 examines the changing ideologies underlying welfare policies, in particular those relating to social security provision – the principal means by which the state has shaped youth and adulthood over time. It examines the basis of government ideologies of 'the family', dependence and independence, and the ways in which these are reflected in the policies of the modern 'market-ized' welfare state. In both these chapters, we review the literature and point to the gaps in our knowledge – gaps which are mainly to do with our understanding of how young people make sense of these structures and follow their individual biographies.

In the next section of the book, we examine the biographies themselves. In Chapter 4, we review young people's social and economic relationships with their families, and identify how these change and develop as young people become adult. In particular, we question the notion of dependence while in the family home. Chapter 5 renders problematic the concept of adulthood, by considering the changing significance of transitional events, and the changing relationship between different transitions (particularly those associated with family and household formation), over time. The chapter explores the circumstances in which independence may be achieved on leaving the family home. Chapter 6 is about the emerging consumer and young people's transitions in relation to markets of consumption, including the housing market. We consider poverty and homelessness in this context.

In the final chapter we bring our argument together and consider its value. We consider the ambiguities and inconsistencies in the way youth is frequently defined, we evaluate attempts to structure dependence and independence, we consider the balance between self-determination in youth and social control of young people by their families and others, and we try to identify how young people become citizens in Britain. We then very briefly consider some ways in which the theoretical framework we have developed could be taken further, and used both as a conceptual basis for the reform of youth policies in Britain, and as a framework for international comparative studies and policy development at a European level.

A lot has been left out of this book. We are aware, in particular, that we have not discussed health, sexuality, crime or many other areas where family and state interventions may structure young people's actions. Many other gaps are not deliberate on our part, but result from the lack of documentary evidence – for example, on young people's perceptions of state policies. In any case, one book is not long enough to cover the whole area. What we have attempted is to bring together some, but not all, of the different strands in young people's lives.

DEFINING 'YOUTH'

Over the ages, the term 'youth', referring to a stage in the life course, has changed and narrowed in meaning. For the last hundred years or so, the term has increasingly been linked with the period known as adolescence, the part of the life course which leads into adulthood. Technically, perhaps, adolescence can itself be defined as the age period between puberty and the legal age of majority, which in Britain is 18 years, and, in theory at least, adolescence is seen as the stage in life during which there is transition from dependent childhood to independent adulthood. But there are enormous problems associated with these terms, some of which are defined according to physical development, some according to social and economic development and some according to legal status. To a great extent, youth and adolescence are social constructions, varying between cultures, and subject to reconstruction over time.

This book has a sub-theme: the significance of age. How important is age as a dimension of inequality structuring transitions (in comparison with other dimensions of inequality)? We consider age in terms of age relations, particularly the relations between generations, or the 'young person's world' and the 'adult world'; we consider age-related legal access to adult citizenship rights; and we consider the relevance of age to the attainment of adult status. The point we want to make, though, is that terms such as 'adolescence' or 'adulthood' are related to life-course events and social relationships, and are relatively loosely associated with physical age. Youth is a process of definition and redefinition, a negotiation enacted between young people and their families, their peers and the institutions of the wider society. This creates a problem of measurement, since – though government policies may be based on age-grading (as Chapters 2 and 3 show) – as social scientists we cannot say at what age young people become adults; nor would we wish to – our concern is with trying to define the ways in which different groups of young people become accepted as 'adult' in different social contexts.

In recent years, because of perceived changes in the structure of transitions, new definitions have emerged. Some German and French sociologists (viz. Zinnekar, 1981; Galland, 1990; Gaiser, 1991) claim to have identified a new 'stage in life', that of 'post-adolescence', a label which they attach to dependence on parents which extends beyond the teenage years. Labels such as these may or may not have value in the British case. In order to determine whether the life course can be broken down into stages in this way, and, if so, whether life stages should be defined by age or by life events, sociological research has to delve more deeply into the meanings behind some of the longer-established expressions which we frequently use, and which we too rarely question.

THEORIES OF YOUTH, FAMILY AND SOCIETY

There seems to have been a problem about locating young people in society, whether as individuals, as a social group, or as family members. There also seems to have been a problem about seeing them as whole individuals, in which their social roles and relationships (student, worker, partner, friend, child) are integrated. To make matters worse, there has been a third problem: that of coping both theoretically and methodologically with the fact that young people are in a process of transition, in a changing society, so that much that may be observed about them one year may no longer be the case in the next year of their lives, partly because they are growing up, and partly because their social context has changed. The sociology of youth through the decades has reflected these three basic problems, but has so far failed to solve them.

In reviewing the sociological literature on young people and their families, one cannot help but be struck by the paucity of work which makes any connection between the two. The sociology of youth, as we shall show, has made little reference to the family context in which most young people grow up. [For example, in examining youth peer groups (see Hall and Jefferson 1976; Mungham and Pearson 1976; Brake, 1980; Frith, 1984), youth policies (Davies, 1986), youth unemployment and employment (see Ashton and Maguire, 1982; Raffe, 1988; Bynner 1990) or youth training and education (see Roberts, 1984; Raffe, 1988; Lee *et al.*, 1990), little reference is made to the family environment or family relationships, except in terms of the influence of fathers' social class on young people's aspirations and orientations (e.g. Carter, 1962, 1966; Ashton and Field, 1976; Willis 1977).] At the same time, the sociology of the family has tended to focus on marital relationships or on the relationships between parents and younger children (see Newson and Newson, 1976; Barrett and McIntosh, 1980; Poster, 1980; Harris, 1983; Morgan, 1985). Little has been written about the relationship between adolescent children and their parents. It is a curious omission, yet one which may reflect a more general ambivalence about the position of young people in British society. Its result is that policy-makers operate in the dark, making assumptions about aspects of young people's behaviour which have not been the subject of empirical research.

Young people in Britain tend to be regarded as a sort of social barometer: their behaviour has been charted over the decades as an index of social ills. This has been a constant theme in the sociology of youth, recently revitalized under the 'New Right', who have quoted rising numbers of births to teenagers, increased delinquency and violence, or teenage drinking and drug-taking, as indicators of a moral decline which has its roots in the breakdown of the traditional values, normally inculcated in traditional family life through parental authority. The 'logic' of this argument has led to policies designed to uphold 'traditional family values', to prevent family breakdown, and to maintain the authority and family obligations of parents. In consequence, the emphasis has been on young people as a problem for the social order, and many sociological investigations have reflected this, featuring evaluations of government initiatives designed to keep young people out of trouble, rather than investigations into the problems of the young, and the ways in which they may learn to cope with the changing circumstances of their social lives as they become older. Policy-related evaluation research into effectiveness of schooling, training programmes, careers service, leisure, and so on, has dominated the sociology of youth, and has produced a focus on the functioning of formal and state-established institutions, such as training schemes, drawing attention away from the more private world and more informal relationships of family life (see, for example, Davies, 1986; Raffe, 1988; Lee *et al.*, 1990; Roberts and Parsell, 1990; and

Table 1.1 Theories of youth in sociology

Structuralist explanations	Individualist explanations
Generation theory	Life-course perspective
Functionalist theory	Individualization thesis
Social reproduction theory	'High modernity'

Chapter 2). The literature on young people and their relationships with their families comes, in contrast, mainly from the realms of psychoanalysis and social psychology (see Coleman, 1961; Erikson, 1968). It assumes normative processes of adolescent development without reference to social contexts.

We would argue that there have been two main theoretical approaches, each of which, in its own way, has made the task of distinguishing youth in a family context more difficult: on the one hand, there have been theories which see the family as a unit, and thus overlook relationships within that unit (here we include the work on macro-social structures deriving from Marx and Weber, and more recently and clearly the work of structural-functionalists such as Parsons and, perhaps, Erikson); at the other extreme, there are new approaches associated with 'post-modernism', which take a 'deconstructionist' view (see Table 1.1). These 'post-modernist' ideas lack a structural framework for understanding the micro-context of family relationships, and, for understanding the interrelationship between the different transitions to adult status. In particular, we consider 'individualization thesis', known in Germany through the work of Beck (1987), which argues that structural frameworks are breaking down to the level of the 'reflexively mobilized' individual. Related work can also be seen to include some examples of the life-course perspective in its application to youth. Somewhere between these two extremes lie the theories currently being developed under the aegis of 'high modernity' (Giddens, 1991).

YOUTH IN THE SOCIAL STRUCTURE

Social-structuralist explanations of youth broadly explain how young people are linked into society. Over time, explanations have considered integration through generation, through social class, through gender or through race and ethnic group. Throughout, there has been concern about whether young people are integrated at all, or whether they live at the margins of society.

Neither Marxian nor Weberian theories offer much of a guide to the exploration of the concept of youth, being concerned with the macro-social structures of class and status, rather than the micro-politics of family life, and indeed both can obscure our understanding, with their emphasis on the family as a closed and private world, with a role in the reproduction of labour, or as a unit of consumption. The generation theories and functionalist perspectives, theories of social reproduction and more recent approaches have tended to contribute either a homogeneous picture of youth, or a static one, or a partial one.

In order to understand the position of young people in the social structure, we have to unravel some of the complexities inherent in the concept of time. In the following pages we shall be talking about generations and about cohorts, about biographical time and about historical time. There is an ongoing confusion in much of the sociological literature about the concept of generation, and this we need to clarify first. The concept has been used in two quite different ways: first, as in Parson's analysis, it is used in the context of kinship relations, to describe the fixed life stages through which people pass during their life course (from childhood to parenthood to grandparenthood, for example) resulting in a conceptual differentiation between older and younger generations in society. It is indeed one of the functions of families, according to Harris (1983) to link individual and historical time through generational kinship structures. In its second sense the concept of generation is used in relation to the historical context into which people are born. This is the way in which Mannheim (1927) used the concept, but as many have since argued (see Kertzer, 1983; Jones, 1991b), his use of the term 'generation' in this way has created much conceptual confusion. A group of people who pass together through historical time are more clearly identified as a 'cohort' rather than as a generation, in sociological terms. Thus, we use the word 'cohort' to label this second meaning, and refer to 'generations' solely in terms of the age divisions which stem, in the main, from kinship relations.

Generation theory

At the end of the nineteenth century, with the heightening of patriotic fervour and nationalism in Europe, the concept of youth was developed and adopted as the embodiment of hope for a better future. Almost immediately, the romantic imagery of the concept was overlaid with concerns, and youth was portrayed as problematic for society. The first social scientist to comment on adolescence was the American G. Stanley Hall, who referred to it both as 'a marvellous new birth' (meaning for society) and also as a period of storm and stress and the age 'when most vicious careers are begun' (Hall, 1904: 325). He thus wrote the somewhat ambiguous scenario which laid a foundation for much of the later research, by simultaneously seeing youth as a force of generational change, and young people as a problem for society.

Anthropologists such as Evans-Pritchard (1951) and Mead (1943) considered whether youth in pre-industrial societies was subject to the same 'storm and stress' as had been identified in Western industrial societies, and found that young people in less complex societies could make a smooth transition to adulthood. This suggested (Reuter, 1937) that it was only in industrial societies, where there was neither appropriate training for adulthood nor a sure place in the social world, that young people faced an adjustment problem and could find themselves temporarily in a 'marginal world'. Basically, the problems experienced by young people were created by society, and were not intrinsic to the nature of youth itself.

It is generations, rather than families, which figure in much of the literature of this period as the context in which young people become adult (viz. Mannheim, 1927), and generation relations are seen as across society as a whole, rather than within the locus of the family and kinship. Thus, when the emphasis in youth research moved to examination of the 'generation war', this referred not to a breakdown of relationships within families, but to a form of adult paranoia about the younger generation. Coleman (1961: 3) suggested that the school system created circumstances in which young people constituted a society among themselves, in other words as a peer group or even generation group, to the detriment of their connections with the rest of adult society. Commentators ranging from Wilson (1970), Musgrove (1974), Friedenberg (1973) to Rex (1972) suggested that the generation struggle was surpassing the class struggle in the 'Affluent Society' of the 1960s. The influence of the family on young people's lives was apparently declining and schools and peer groups were taking over.

These studies failed to take account of an essential argument in Mannheim's (1927) earlier analysis, that members of cohorts ('generations' in his terminology), though located in the same historical time, were still differentiated by their geographical location and position in the social structure into 'generation-units'. Historical events were experienced differently by people in different social and spatial locations. Equally, the impact that young people had on the wider society varied according to their social grouping. As studies of youth cultures developed, new theories of social reproduction refuted much of this earlier 'generational' approach, and rediscovered social divisions among the young, as we shall show.

Functionalist theory

Much of the focus in functionalist theories was on the roles of family members, mainly mothers and fathers, in educating their young for their future adult lives, and in particular ensuring that they achieve their own prescribed social roles as workers in the labour market or in the home. The theory of 'primary socialization' emphasized the importance of families as 'the "factories" which produce human personalities' (Parsons, 1956: 16). According to this theory, families taught their children to conform to social norms and learn culturally prescribed social and familial roles. For the process to be successful, it was deemed necessary for the child to be dependent on its parents, at least temporarily, in order to learn from the parents' role models. Parsons recognized, however, that in time, the family must fulfil another function, and 'help in emancipating the child from his dependency on the family' (Parsons, 1956: 19).

As societies have become increasingly complex, institutions have taken over many of the roles of parents, not just in terms of their children's education, but with regard to their health and welfare as well. There was concern about the decline in family life and the loss of function of the family back in the 1950s (just as there is currently in the 1980s and 1990s), but this was refuted by Parsons (1956: 9), who argued that the role of the family in socialization had merely become more specialized. The structure of family relations was thus still shaped by the needs of (capitalist/patriarchal) industrial society, just as it had been before the expansion of education and the development of the welfare state. Girls were brought up to be wives and mothers, boys to be heads of household and breadwinners, for the normative nuclear families of the future.

In an industrial society, primary socialization within the family is unable to prepare young people adequately for their future social roles, and so, according to Eisenstadt (1956) and Reuter (1937) it was necessary to supplement it with secondary socialization in institutions set up by the state, such as schools. Secondary socialization of a more 'subverting' kind could also be a function of the peer group (Coleman, 1961). Through membership of the school or peer group, the adolescent (Parsons, 1961: 446):

> both transcends [*sic*] his familial identification in favour of a more independent one and comes to identify a more differentiated status within the new system.

Secondary socialization was therefore seen, like primary socialization, to have a role in helping with the development of independence from the family, and the institutions of the state were thus taking over many of the responsibilities of parents in this respect.

There are times when the socializing institutions of the family and the state stop working in harmony. Parsons (1973: 41) suggests that in such circumstances, 'where the individual is subject to conflicting pressures that are impossible to fulfil all at once', anomie can result. Adolescents were described as feeling unwanted by the world of adults, and confused about what was expected of them. Erikson described how young people could be bewildered by their own feeling of incapacity to assume the role which society is forcing upon them (Erikson, 1968: 121), but it was also argued (see, for example, Toffler, 1970) that given that future roles were so uncertain, it is no longer possible to know what role a young person is being socialized *for*.

Explanations of youth tend to be historically specific. During the 1960s and 1970s, functionalist theories became discredited. They assumed the possibility of smooth transitions to adulthood (cf. Reuter, 1937) and could only explain the observed 'marginalization' of youth in terms of failure in the process of socialization. The theory may once have been appropriate, but did not hold up well in the face of the social changes which had occurred by the late 1960s, with the emergence of youth subcultures, the increased demands of young people for freedom of expression, the demands of women for equality, and the challenges to the notion that normative roles were there to be filled. There was a demand for change, and for self-determination.

During the 1980s, it became increasingly clear that simple unitary models of the transition to adulthood could no longer be defended. The nature of transitions to adulthood continued to change in the climate of economic recession (with industrial decline and widespread unemployment) and as a result of the policies of the Thatcher Government. The increase in youth unemployment and youth training schemes meant that for many early school leavers there was no longer a simple transition from school to work. There had also been changes in patterns of family formation, which meant that there was more cohabitation and less association between marriage and childbirth. The availability of cheap rented accommodation was diminishing with the privatization of housing stock, and the transition to independent housing was becoming more difficult. Each transition was becoming more complex and less standardized.

What is the point of socializing someone for manual work, when industry is in decline; or socializing young women into the role of mothers when they may not have children, and even if they do, will probably need to have dual roles as mothers and as paid workers; or socializing young people into work, when their entry into the labour market is delayed by training schemes and job shortages? It is perhaps this uncertainty about the aims of socialization in the modern world which leads to such conflicts of expectation and demands between families involved in primary socialization and the other institutions of the state which are concerned with secondary socialization. When the shape of the future is in doubt, young people themselves are unlikely to be any clearer than their parents or their teachers what they are aiming for (and thus are more likely to turn to their peer group for support and guidance). In a changing world, the models set by the older generation are often no longer relevant, and some young people will be increasingly likely to be marginalized (as perhaps are their families?). Parsons took a life-cycle rather than life-course approach; in other words, though he focused on process, he failed to take account of the ways in which movement from one life-stage to another might be subject to structural change over historical time, and indeed of the variation of experience within cohorts according to their social and geographical locations.

Theories of social reproduction

When sociologists began to examine the youth cultures of the 1960s, they found that though they were expressed in the peer group, they were often based on values which were shared between young people and their parents (Berger, 1963), and that young people were basically conformist rather than in opposition to adult society (Zweig, 1963; Friedenberg, 1973; and even Parsons, 1973). The later studies of youth subcultures in the 1970s and 1980s (see Brake, 1980, for an overview), stemmed from the resulting need to move beyond a generational analysis in the study of youth, and to introduce a social class perspective. Marxist scholars such as Althusser (1971) provided a structural framework for the theories of social and cultural reproduction which developed in Britain.

In the work of Paul Willis (1977) and the Centre for Contemporary Cultural Studies (CCCS), the social class basis of youth cultures was defined, *sub*cultures were identified, and young people were seen in a class (and much later, gender and race) perspective. Their work developed from new debates within the sociology of deviance. The emphasis was on the reproduction of power structures such as social class inequalities through the peer group. Although these writers were reacting against the functionalist perspectives put forward by Coleman and Parsons, they nevertheless still reflected some of them. The work of Willis (1977) and Corrigan (1979), for example, emphasized the importance of the peer group and the school system in the reproduction of work roles from generation to generation. Willis described the reproduction of manual labour through alienation from school culture and positive reinforcement, or socialization, by the peer group. Interest in anti-school working-class subcultures culminated in a whole series of research projects (see Hall and Jefferson, 1976; Mungham and Pearson, 1976). The theories can be seen in many ways to integrate many functionalist ideas within a structural perspective.

These studies were, however, quite different in focus from the studies of youth cultures of the 1960s. The move had been away from seeing youth as 'a class in itself' to seeing young people's actions as rooted in the social class structure of society. Though the emphasis was on male working-class subcultures, there were important developments within this framework, for example, by Richard Jenkins (1983) who examined heterogeneity within the male working class. But there were limitations within this perspective too. It produced a very partial analysis of youth, concentrating on peer group activity, on the working class, and on young men. Women, the middle class and 'conventional' young people were largely overlooked.

Family life did not figure prominently in the bulk of this research – not surprisingly, since it was focused on the non-private lives of young men (Hall and Jefferson, 1976; Willis, 1977). It was only when the invisibility of young women in subcultural studies was investigated (see McRobbie and Garber, 1976) that the function of the home and the family began to be recognized. Even then, this was only as a locus for more private female peer group activity (including 'bedroom culture'), rather than an attempt to study the relationship between young people and their parents. It was somewhat later that Chris Griffin (1985) replicated Willis's (1977) study, focusing instead on young women and examining the role of family life and female peer groups as means of socializing young women into their future roles as wives, mothers or workers. It is in the construction of gender identities in particular, that family life, through socialization, reproduces structural inequalities. The conceptual division of the social world into its public and its private spheres bears little relation to reality and cannot therefore help us understand how young people become adult.

There was criticism from feminists, and others representing disadvantaged groups, that social reproduction theories were based on unquestioned implicit assumptions, and that theories based on class reproduction could not comfortably take account of other dimensions of stratification, such as gender, race, and disability (and we might add sexuality to this list). From the 1970s, these critics began to abandon their attempts to accommodate, for example, feminism within Marxism (viz. Beechey, 1977), and instead they produced theories of reproduction of other power structures, including patriarchy (Walby, 1989), heterosexism (Rich, 1981), racism (Solomos, 1988), and disability (Walker, 1982), all of which were perceived as co-existing with the class structures of industrial capitalism, though not necessarily along the same axis. The introduction of more and more dimensions to the concept of the social structure of inequality can lead to the demolition of social-structural macro-theory, and indeed eventually to individualization. Furthermore, the approach can lose sight of the dynamic inherent both in youth and in the social structures which give it context.

DE-CONSTRUCTING YOUTH

In recent years, there have been new perspectives in sociology, responding to the need for a holistic approach which re-unites the public and private worlds. The life-course approach does this, and allows the examination of transitions to adulthood in terms of the relationship between different aspects of the transition, such as that between employment and family formation. It also allows an exploration of the complexities underlying concepts such as dependency and independence in youth.

Life-course perspective

The life course is the biography of the individual, the product of the relationship between self and others within the age/date relationship (see Jones, 1991). Hareven (1982: 6) best describes the approach:

> A life course perspective views the interrelationships between individual and collective family behaviour as they constantly change over people's lives and in the context of historical conditions. The life course approach is concerned with the movement of individuals over their own lives and through historical time and with the relationship of family members to each other as they travel through personal and historical time.

It was only with the emergence of studies of the life course that the focus in youth research has shifted and a more holistic approach to understanding young people has been adopted, in which their relationships with their families, their peers, the labour market, and so on, can be integrated within a biographical approach. In the work of Hutson and Jenkins (1989), Allatt and Yeandle (1986), Griffin (1985), Wallace (1987a), Jones (1986; 1990a), and much of the work emanating from the Economic and Social Research Council (ESRC) 16–19 Initiative (Bynner, 1991), the lives of young people in their households and in the labour market has been investigated. Youth can be seen as a series of processes of transition to adult life, roughly parallel longitudinal processes which take place in different spheres, such as at home or in the labour market, but which must be understood together because they relate closely to one another. The biographical approach requires that the lives of the young are seen as an integrated whole. Heinz (1988) points out that it is possible to see at the same time both the structuring effects of social institutions on the life course and the way in which individuals negotiate their way through these institutions. The perspective integrates process and structure in the manner advocated by Jones (1988) and links individual time with historical time.

A consequence of the life-course approach is that it becomes poss-ible to draw together two areas of sociology which have rarely been united before: the sociology of youth and the sociology of family life. Just as the family context has tended to be absent from youth re-search, so young people have been missing from much of the research into family life.

The sociology of family life, while it claims to have opened up the 'black box' of the family, imposed by 'structuralist' theories which saw the family as a unit in its relations with the external world, has still barely focused on the relations between young people and their parents, and the economic roles of young people in households. It has instead concentrated on spouse relations, or the parenting of young children. Much of the work has, however, examined inequalities within households, concentrating mainly on unequal access of hus-bands and wives to goods and household income, and the work has helped inform government policies with regard to the taxation of marriage partners (see, for example, Pahl, 1983; Brannen and Wilson, 1987; Morris, 1990), but the part that older children play in the family economy has been neglected as a research topic, as Finch (1989) has shown. Children are regarded as dependants and therefore not intrin-sically important in economic terms.

These new approaches to the study of family life suggest that family members, far from adopting structurally-prescribed familial roles, as functionalist theories suggest, are involved in a constant process of negotiating their relationships (see, for example, Newson and News-on 1976; or Prout 1988, on younger children's negotiations with their parents). This means that as young people grow up, their relation-ships with their parents can shift, as new negotiations occur. In other words, people do not just grow older: they change and their relation-ships change as well. Unfortunately, some of the research in this area still fails to take account of the process of growing up, and the nego-tiations which are observed are not seen to be structured by changing age relations. It may be that once micro-processes in families are examined, it is hard to keep sight of the macro-inequalities which may structure them. For the same reason, it is common in studies which examine the detail of family relations not to site themselves in the broader social inequalities of class, gender and race.

There are therefore new dangers: in examining all aspects of people's lives, we could end up, through a process of infinite reduction, looking at individuals rather than social groups. In an era of post-modernism in sociology, perspectives have increasingly become 'de-constructionist', to the extent of describing a 'fragmented self' where there is no acting agent (see Giddens, 1991, for a critique). Some examples of the life-course perspective have lost sight of structural inequalities and the continuities of social reproduction.

Individualization thesis

Ulrich Beck has been influential in European sociology in putting forward his 'individualization thesis'. Though derived as a general thesis on German society, it has been frequently applied to the study of youth. The crux of his argument (Beck, 1986; 1987) is that there has been fragmentation of the established structures of reproduction in society, in terms of education, work and family forms, and a breakdown of traditional institutions, with the result that individual social roles are no longer clear. Giddens has produced a similar argument, suggesting that in the 'post-traditional social universe', an infinite range of potential courses of action (and attendant risks) is open to individuals and collectivities. Risks are increased at all levels – not just the lower socio-economic levels – in what Beck refers to as a 'risk society'. According to Giddens (1991: 28), living in this 'risk society'

> means living with a calculative attitude to the open possibilities of action, positive and negative, with which, as individuals and globally, we are confronted in a continuous way in our contemporary social existence.

Beck argues that, in their efforts to decrease their personal risks, individuals have turned away from the old class cultures, which have nothing to offer any more, and can no longer gain support from the traditional networks of the family; they thus have to try to achieve their personal ambitions in individualized ways. According to Beck, the structures of inequality (class, gender, race, and so on) may no longer be as over-arching and life becomes a 'biographical project'. A picture is thus painted of individuals seeking to achieve their own aims in a highly competitive world. Family life has changed and its traditional forms no longer exist (an issue which we discuss in Chapter 4); within the family, its members are involved in their own individual patterns of work and consumption. This view contrasts with Marxian and Weberian theories which see the family as a unit, either of production or consumption, headed and thus defined by a male breadwinner. It also contrasts with more recent studies which commented on the level of cooperation within families (e.g. Pahl, 1984).

Within Beck's thesis, the young person within the family is thus forcibly 'emancipated', but emancipation brings risks.

Apart from changes to the family structure, there have also been, according to the individualization thesis, changes in the power relationships within families. The emergence of Children's Rights movements, for example, have led to increased awareness of children as individuals and to some loss of parental power and control (Hartmann, 1987; Hermanns, 1987). Competition for jobs in the labour market has led to a breakdown of traditional family and community ties, and a young person's entry into the labour market is likely to put particular strain on family relationships. Individualization may lead to increased choice and autonomy (Hartmann, 1987), or to increasing risk of downward mobility, uncertainty and stress (Heinz *et al.*, 1987). The thesis was developed for the West German case, though it has also been applied elsewhere in Europe, and since similar changes have been occurring in Britain, parts of the thesis could be argued for Britain too.

High modernity and life trajectories

Giddens' (1991) study of modernity and the self contains many of the same starting points as Beck but puts them into a different theoretical construction, drawing on literature from the realms of psychoanalysis and social psychology as well as sociology. He too talks of increased risks and increased chances, but unlike Beck he continues to stress structural constraints. Thus, arguing against post-modernist claims that the new era is characterized by fragmentation of modern institutions, he suggests instead that the unifying features of modern institutions are just as central in the present age as the dis-aggregating ones (Giddens, 1991: 27). So, for example, when discussing the continued exclusion of women from full participation in society, he says (1991: 106):

> Women today have the nominal opportunity to follow a whole variety of opportunities and chances: yet in a masculinist culture, many of these avenues remain effectively foreclosed. Moreover, to embrace those which do exist, women have to abandon their earlier 'fixed' identities in a more thorough-going way than do men. In other words, they experience the openness of late modernity in a fuller, yet more contradictory, way.

Giddens, too, places his discussion in the context of changing family relations, but here again he has a different interpretation from that of Beck. He quotes the work of Stacey (1990) who shows that individuals experiencing the unravelling of traditional family patterns, and the concomitant risks associated with this experience, are nevertheless constructing new forms of family relation in a 'massive process of institutional reconstitution'. New extended families ('recombinant families') are being created, though no longer organized in terms of pre-established gender divisions; divorce is being mobilized as a resource, drawing together new family networks. This process, far from resulting in individualization, thus creates new forms, and individuals 'appear not as withdrawing from the outer social world but engaging boldly with it' (Giddens, 1991: 177).

Giddens's argument is that life is not so much a 'biographical project' as a 'reflexive' one. Life transitions, such as the transition from adolescent to adult, demand the exploration and construction of the altered self as part of a reflexive process of connecting personal and social change (1991: 33). Nevertheless, as the above quotation about women shows, structures still provide some parameters.

Though Giddens has focused his analysis on the trajectories of adult lives, rather than on trajectories through youth, it seems to us that his work contributes in some part to our original specification, for a sociology of youth which could combine holism, process and the analysis of inequality in an integrated approach.

RE-CONSTRUCTING YOUTH

So far there have been two sides to the sociology of youth – on the one hand the social-structural (traditional 'modernist'?) view, which can be over-deterministic, and on the other hand ideas of individualization, which tend to over-stress self-determination. We need to allow ourselves some theoretical eclecticism: to pull out of the earlier theories the parts that are relevant to the modern world, and to acknowledge the contribution of more contemporary views, using the best of both sources as the foundation stones for a new theory of youth.

There have been attempts to create a theoretical framework for understanding both the structural context of youth and the process involved in transitions to adulthood, but to combine process with structure is a complex process. A study by Jones (1986, 1987a, 1988) sought to examine transitions to adulthood in the context of social mobility, as young people move into adult social class positions, and developed a thesis that young people's class trajectories, rather than their (or their fathers' or mothers') current occupational class, were the chief determinants of their life chances. Wallace's (1987a) study of young people used the concept of employment careers to differentiate between social groups. Within the ESRC 16–19 Initiative (see Bynner, 1990), the notion of career trajectories was introduced, as a means of differentiating between unequal groups of young people. Increasingly, then, we are seeking to incorporate a longitudinal dimension to the concept of youth, and at the same time to understand youth as a differentiated process.

We are at a stage in the British sociology of youth where new theoretical frameworks need to be developed. We are trying to hold together the concept of youth as a process and part of the life course, with increasing awareness of heterogeneity and diversity. A coherent theory is needed to help us understand the intra-family and wider social processes which shape youth and the transitions which comprise this part of the life course, but the theory should also allow us to understand how ideologies of youth develop and are imposed through state policies. This means that we need to understand historical change as well as individual life-course transitions. Furthermore, we increasingly need to be able to generalize from the national example to cross-national comparisons. This is the agenda that we set ourselves in this book.

YOUTH AND CITIZENSHIP

The concept of citizenship seems to us to offer an opportunity to redefine and re-structure the concept of youth. It implies a package of rights and responsibilities for individuals in welfare capitalist societies which are implicitly transmitted with age. Youth can be seen as the period during which the transition to citizenship, that is, to full participation in society, occurs. However, citizenship offers a more useful framework than adulthood for understanding the 'end product' of youth: it allows us to consider process, but at the same time allows us to consider inequality – while citizenship *rights* are gradually acquired during youth, *access* to these rights, including to full participation in society, is still determined by the social structures of inequality such as social class, gender, race, disability and so on. Three main issues therefore concern us here. First, what is citizenship? Second, how does a young person become a citizen? And third, to what extent is citizenship achievable for all?

In its formulation by Marshall (1950), citizenship has developed over time in Britain so that by the middle of the twentieth century it had three elements – civil, political and social – which together produced the right to participation in the community (see Barbalet, 1988). Civil citizenship, including the rights to personal freedom, to property, and to protection against the state, developed in the eighteenth century, and is acquired through the rule of law; political rights began to develop in the nineteenth century and are conferred through the electoral process and universal adult suffrage; social citizenship, the right to the prevailing living standard in society, is realized through the education, health, housing and social welfare systems and developed largely through the creation of the welfare state after the Second World War (Marshall, 1950). In Marshall's own words (1949: 74):

> The civil element is composed of the rights necessary for individual freedom – liberty of the person, freedom of speech, thought and faith, the right to own property and to conclude valid contracts, and the right to justice ... By the political element, I mean the right to participate in the exercise of political power, as a member of a body invested with political authority or as an elector of the members of such a body. The corresponding institutions are parliament and the councils of local government. By the social element, I mean the whole range from the right to a modicum of economic welfare and security to the right to share to the full in the social heritage and to live the life of a civilised being according to the standards prevailing in the society.

Social citizenship must be provided by the state. Despite this safety net, however, as Barbalet (1988) points out, access to citizenship is not universal, since it is determined not only by legal rights but also by the ability of individuals to mobilize their personal resources. Structures of stratification are thus unlikely to be eroded by the development of citizenship, though, according to Marshall (1950) conflicts may thus be set up.

Marshall's classic account was imbued with post-war optimism. He saw a world which was moving towards greater and greater equality, reflected in the provisions of the welfare state: incomes policy, social insurance, the development of the national health service, the extension of universal education, and housing policy. The move from Poor Law to welfare state represented the final act in the evolution of social citizenship (Marshall, 1952).

Citizenship and dependence

T.H. Marshall focused on the position of men in society, and the relationship between citizenship and social class (rather than other dimensions of stratification, such as gender, race or age). The issue of differential access to basic rights of citizenship according to race has since been raised (Smith, 1989; Harrison, 1991). Recent attempts to apply the concept of citizenship to women (see Lister, 1990; Summers, 1991), raise the question whether women can achieve full participation as citizens as long as they remain, in marriage at least, economically dependent on men. Indeed our understanding of Marshall's argument is that property rights, including ownership of one's own labour, have been crucial in determining other citizenship rights. The implicit idea in Marshall's construction was that citizenship would be granted to dependants, such as women and children, indirectly through the main head of household. Lister argues that until women are allowed full economic independence, including recognition of their role as carers, then full citizenship will continue to be withheld from them.

The debate on citizenship has not yet been explicitly applied to young people. There are some parallels in the situations of women and young people in the family (including of course the fact that they are over-lapping groups), because of their actual or assumed position of economic dependence on the head of household. Lister draws our attention to the ways in which women's dependence is structured in the public and private sectors, through the domestic division of labour, and through the organization of paid employment and state provisions (see also Summers, 1991). Marshall (1952) took no account of the problematic relationship between citizenship and dependency (Pascall, 1986), an issue which has to be addressed when the concept of citizenship is applied to women, young people and the older population. Lister argues that economic independence is central to claims for full citizenship – but that instead of demanding independence, we argue for interdependence and say that the dichotomy between dependence and independence is a false one (Land, 1989; also, with regard to young people, Jones, 1992).

Interdependence and sharing between men and women, depends, Lister argues (1990: 446–7), on equality. Thus she argues that:

> True interdependence and sharing between individual men and women will not be possible so long as the economic and power relationships underpinning their interdependence are so unequal and so long as women's unpaid work as carers is devalued.

The economic dependency of women, either on their male partners or on the state, contravenes all ideas of citizenship, even when the women are in full-time work caring for children and servicing a male workforce (thus freeing the adult males in the family from economic dependence). Unpaid work in the home and responsibilities within the family 'don't count' as far as citizenship is concerned. Summers (1991) points out that child care must be taken into account before most women can gain equality in citizenship: this implies not only acknowledgement that women care for the sick and elderly, but also recognition in economic terms for taking on these tasks. Instead, as Graham (1983) indicates, what goes on within families is seen to be outside the structure of public rights and obligations.

These arguments can apply to young people too: school work, helping in the home, even part-time paid work, are not recognized as work in our society and do not carry any rights (such as National Insurance, trade union membership, or employment protection). Full participation (rights and access to them) in society is, as Marshall (1950) indicated, dependent on personal resources and position in the social structure; and thus, following Lister (1990), also depends on the achievement of economic independence: this applies to young people of both sexes. Economic independence must be achieved if they are to be allowed full participation in society. In the case of young people, as with women, the process of economic emancipation has to be enacted first of all within the family of origin, though, as we shall see, emancipation within the family has only limited recognition in the outside world. Full economic independence in youth is achieved through the structures of the labour market and the welfare state.

Whereas Marshall provides what to many observers is an evolutionary account of citizenship, the moment it is applied to young people the concept takes on a 'life-course' dimension. What he described as happening at the level of society over historical time, appears also to apply at the level of the individual during the life course. The gradual acquisition of citizenship rights and duties characterizes the period of youth. Legal rights and responsibilities are age structured: some civil rights, such as the right to work, and civil duties, such as responsibility under the law, are acquired before the age of majority; political rights come, for the most part, with the age of majority; social citizenship rights, including the right to social security, are far more problematic and access to different rights is spread by legislation over a wide age range. This life-course perspective on citizenship is the main underlying theme of this book. Turner has also now emphasized the impact of ageing on social membership and indicates that the 'reciprocity–maturation curve' (increases in status through education, employment or inheritance leading to property ownership and household and family formation) is central to his understanding of citizenship (Turner, 1991).

We are attempting to take a longitudinal approach to citizenship, and to consider youth as a period during which citizenship rights and responsibilities are accrued. Two further points, developed by other writers with regard to citizenship at the level of society, will be seen to be particularly relevant to this analysis. First, citizenship rights are not a homogeneous or unified set of social arrangements (Giddens, 1982) and we shall see how conflicts and ambiguities can occur at the individual level because of this. Second, that the societal development of different rights is not necessarily either even or parallel, nor indeed is it irreversible (Turner, 1990), and we shall apply this concept at the individual level as well.

The acquisition of citizenship rights during youth is complex and uneven. Political citizenship, with the right to vote or take part in the legal process as a juror, may come at 18 years, but social citizenship is less easy to define and appears harder to achieve. We shall see that increasingly in modern Britain it is only full-time paid employment which can bring economic independence and the right to a stake in national civic life. Women and children are assumed to gain these rights by proxy, through their husbands or fathers, at least in a two-parent family, but adolescents and young adults are in a problematic situation between dependence and independence. Every piece of legislation which extends the period of dependence in childhood, defers not only adult status, but also the status of citizen in the wider social world. The longer full-time paid employment is withheld from young people, the more training schemes they are expected to enrol on, the longer they are expected to remain dependent on their parents – the more the goal of citizenship, with its obligations as well as rights, seems to be retreating into the distance.

The concept of citizenship is a political issue, and not only the structuring, but also the definition of citizenship is therefore subject to political change. Citizenship contains two elements which tend to be variously stressed in political rhetoric: rights and responsibilities. Thus, as Lister (1990) indicates, on the one hand the political right emphasizes the *obligations* of a citizen (to be independent, to care for the elderly and sick, to give to charity) – 'active citizenship' of this kind tends to be part of the rhetoric of Conservative governments; while on the other hand the political centre and left parties tend to emphasize citizens' *rights*, including that of participation in the democratic process.

And the debate continues. The concept of citizenship rights is now increasingly extended beyond the framework produced by Marshall to include consumer rights. Harrison (1991) points out that discussion of social policy and the welfare state in practice often concerns the control, maintenance, management and organization of consumption for households, groups and individuals. Thus the social division of welfare is crucial in regulating access to citizenship and it is important also to consider citizenship in terms of consumption. Harrison tentatively suggests that privatized forms of social provision and access to 'choices' in markets might amount to alternative forms of citizenship in modern-day Britain. 'Consumer citizenship' appears also to be a focus of Prime Minister John Major's 'Citizen's Charter', and the current political rhetoric is about the rights of individuals to a decent level of public services, though whether the concept has to do with individual rights, or is more focused on how to control the privatized (de-nationalized) industries, such as transport and communication services, remains to be seen.

In our discussion of youth and citizenship we will address a number of different themes:

- Civil – political – social
- Rights and responsibilities
- Inequality of access
- Dependence and independence
- Citizenship by proxy?
- Consumer citizenship.

We shall be examining issues relating to the civil, political and social elements within the citizenship concept as formulated by Marshall; we shall consider the ways in which rights and responsibilities are acquired in youth; throughout, we shall be examining differential access to these rights, as a way of conceptualizing inequality in youth; we will consider the question of direct rights and rights obtained by proxy; we will examine the structuring of economic dependence and independence, and consider the relationship between these and the concepts of control and emancipation; finally, we shall evaluate the idea of consumer citizenship as it applies to young people.

What is now much needed, in order to understand current problems like homelessness and the effects of youth unemployment and training programmes, is an explanation of youth which examines the concepts of dependence and independence and which shows how young people gain citizenship in our society. It involves understanding the process of emancipation and it involves a holistic approach to young people in the various spheres of their lives (the public and the private). It also, and indeed crucially, involves understanding the inequalities which divide young people and which determine their life chances (e.g. inequalities resulting from social class, race, gender, or the region in which they live). Only then will we have the basis for engaging in debate with policy-makers and advising on policies in the future.

The problem we set ourselves in trying to clarify these issues is a difficult one. The confusions associated with definitions of youth and adulthood, with dependence and independence, are exemplified in British legislation defining the rights and obligations of young people. Yet state interventions such as these are structuring the period of youth – though they are not always successful, as we shall see, partly because the ideologies underlying different pieces of government policy may conflict with one another, sometimes for political reasons, and partly because individuals and their families are often resistant to imposed change.

2

STRUCTURING ECONOMIC

DEPENDENCY

Access to the full rights of citizenship – civil, political and social –
depends on the achievement of economic independence. Thus, it has
been argued, women will never achieve full citizenship as long as they
are economically dependent, within their families, on men (Lister
1991; Summers, 1991). These, and other writers, have criticized the
conceptual separation of the social world into its public and private
spheres. We shall see in Chapter 4 the very close association in youth
between economic transitions in the public world and negotiation of
social and economic relationships in the private world of family life.
Lister (1991, quoting Fraser, 1990) points out, moreover, that the treatment of everything outside the private sphere as 'public' conflates three
distinct issues: the state, the official economy of paid employment and
arenas of political discourse. The state determines the social allocation
of citizenship rights, and we shall be turning to this in Chapter 3. Here
we focus on access to the formal economy of paid employment and the
transition to economic independence through the structures of education, training and the labour market. These structures are themselves in
transition over historical time, and major changes have occurred in
recent times, specifically in the post-war period – changes which have
defined and re-defined economic status in youth.

The wage has traditionally been important as the means through
which economic independence has been achieved in youth, and has
been described as 'the key to citizenship' (Pateman, 1989, quoted in
Lister, 1991). Leaving home, getting married and other transition
events associated with adulthood have depended upon getting a job.
The expansion of education and training and the rise in unemployment over the last 20 years has meant, however, that fewer and fewer
young people go straight into employment on leaving school. Instead

of becoming workers and earning a viable wage from employment, they are increasingly to be found within various 'transitional economic statuses', dependent upon grants, allowances, help from parents or other support. In this chapter we explore the way in which transitional economic statuses have been introduced and become standardized as part of the transition process in youth, and the ways in which internal forms of stratification are generated within these new statuses. Finally, we consider the implications for equality and economic independence in youth. The discussion raises a question about young people's position in society: if they cannot become full wage-earners, how and when can they become full citizens?

THE TRANSITION FROM SCHOOL INTO THE LABOUR MARKET

There is no longer a direct transition from school to work. Official statistics, shown in Figure 2.1, indicate the way in which the destinations of 16-year-olds in England and Wales have changed since 1976, though the shifts in patterns of transition reflect much longer-term trends. The figure shows an increasing tendency for young people to remain in full-time education beyond the age of 16 years. The numbers of young people going straight into employment at the minimum school-leaving age have fallen dramatically from 53 per cent in 1976 to 15 per cent in 1986 (although they apparently rose to 20 per cent in 1988, when 'other destinations' and 'employed' categories were combined). Youth Training did not exist in 1976 but has emerged as a category, absorbing over a quarter of 16-year-olds by 1986. Unemployment among 16-year-olds rose from 7 per cent in 1976 to 12 per cent in 1986, but its full extent is concealed by changes in the method of calculating the numbers unemployed, and by the arrangements for income maintenance for this age group (see Chapter 3). Altogether, then, patterns of transition from school have been extended, with young people remaining economically dependent on the state or their families for longer periods. These changes have taken place partly because of rising unemployment, but also partly because education and training have changed in significance and reshaped patterns of transition into the labour market.

The most common way to characterize the school to work transition in British studies has been in terms of the reproduction of social classes. A range of studies has considered how social class of origin was reproduced through the education system to create stability of the class structure inter-generationally (see for example Ashton and Field, 1976; Bowles and Gintis, 1976; Halsey *et al.*, 1980). The

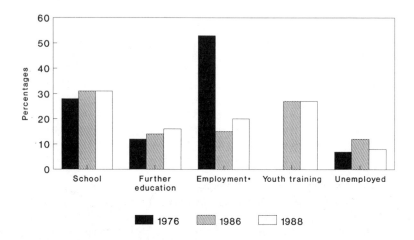

Figure 2.1   Destinations of 16-year-olds
Source: DES Statistics & Social Trends, HMSO.
Note: The asterisk indicates inclusion of 'other' destinations in 1988.

extension and re-shaping of the transition process means that mechanisms of reproduction have been transformed. Changes in the occupational structure during the 1970s and 1980s, following unemployment and de-regulation of the labour market, mean that 'universal models' of regulated class transition are no longer as appropriate. Social class membership has to be considered in the contexts both of inter-generational and of intra-generational social mobility, in other words, as part of a complex dynamic involving individual class careers within a changing social structure (Goldthorpe, 1980; Jones, 1987b). Other dimensions of stratification, such as gender and race were also inadequately accounted for in these earlier models and more recent studies have emphasized the importance of patriarchy and racism (Griffin, 1985; Solomos, 1988; Walby, 1989; Williams, 1989) and other issues, including regional inequality, disability and sexual orientation (Ashton and Maguire, 1982; Walker, 1982), all of which affect economic status and the structuring of the education to labour market transition. We now also have to take into account new forms of stratification internally generated by the training and educational systems themselves. Young people's positions in the consumer market and in the domestic economy may add a further dimension to the ways in which they are situated within the social world (see Chapters 4 and 6). The way in which all these dimensions of inequality intersect is important in understanding the social identity of young people during their transition into the labour market.

According to some arguments, the extension of this transition has been associated with increasingly differentiated career pathways (Heinz, 1987; Heinz *et al.*, 1987). The profusion of training and educational opportunities has led to increased 'choice', but has also made young people more self-conscious about choosing their routes through the system; it is said that they have to be more 'reflexively mobilized', more 'individualized', perhaps. Along with increased choice comes increased risk as outcomes become more uncertain – training, for example, does not necessarily lead to a job. We will explore the validity of these arguments in terms of the trends in education, training and work in Britain.

Before we can consider choice, it is important to establish what structures and controls it. In this chapter we will examine the way in which pathways out of school have been transformed by the structures of the education, training and labour systems. In the following pages we consider the expansion which has taken place in education and training, and the forms of stratification which are emerging. We will identify new intermediate statuses which have emerged, and consider the implications for the independence or dependency of young people in terms of their biographies.

THE CHANGING TRANSITION INTO THE LABOUR MARKET

The normative model of transition from school to work involved finishing education and then going into work – for most groups of young people this took place when they were in their teenage years and enabled them to earn a wage which in turn made possible other kinds of transition (leaving home, finding accommodation or starting a family). For most of the twentieth century this transition, though clearly stratified by social class, was mainly structured by the age of leaving school. From the time that education was made compulsory by law in the nineteenth century, the minimum age of leaving school (and legally being allowed to start full-time employment) has been moving upwards – from 11 to 13 years at the end of the nineteenth century, to 14 years in 1918, to 15 years with the passing of the Education Act 1944. This Act, which established a framework for schooling in the post-war period, was intended to lay the foundations for a system of universal access to secondary education based on ability to learn rather than ability to pay. In 1972, the school-leaving age was raised again, to 16 years, following demand from educational advisers over a long period. The fear of rising unemployment in the 1970s also played a part in this. The legislation has had the effect of continually extending young people's dependence on their families and thus delaying their transition to adulthood in economic terms.

The age at which a young person leaves full-time education and starts work still reflects social class differences but these are not as discernible as they were in the past. The importance of class in regulating these transitions was more obvious before the 1970s; this is partly because studies tended to examine class as the main stratifying variable. Middle-class young people were then more likely to stay on at school, acquire qualifications and find extended training in the labour market than those from working-class homes (Ashton and Field, 1976). Higher educational opportunities were similarly pursued mainly by a middle-class minority. Young people from working-class homes were more likely to enter work directly on leaving school, though apprentices in some trades were able to continue their education through 'day release'. A number of studies at the time documented social class differences in patterns of school and work entry (Carter, 1962, 1966; Robbins Report, 1963; Maizels, 1970; Ashton and Field, 1976). These studies suggested that traditional working-class cultures undervalued educational achievement, and recommended that more working-class young people should be encouraged to improve their prospects through staying on at school and gaining more qualifications. The evidence indicated that social stratification occurred before young people entered the labour market but also continued once they were in it (Roberts, 1984; Ainley, 1988). Patterns of transition at this time were thus regulated in various ways by position within the class structure.

Other dimensions of stratification have been less well documented until recently: gender, for one. Girls' education was not felt to be as important as boys' during the first part of the twentieth century because they were destined for roles as housewives and mothers. Apprenticeships were mostly held by males: in 1950, for example, 33 per cent of males but only 8 per cent of females were in full-time apprenticeships (Roberts, 1984). However, both gender and social class are cross-cut by other forms of stratification and these have been relatively neglected. Black young people also faced disadvantages in the labour market and the school system, and their experiences are further stratified: for example by ethnicity, those of Indian origin being more likely to hold higher qualifications than either white people or those of Pakistani or Bangladeshi origin, or by gender, with Afro-Caribbean women more likely to hold higher qualifications than either Afro-Caribbean or white men (*Social Trends 21*, 1991). Even with higher qualifications many members of ethnic minority groups still experience discrimination in the labour market and may end up with lower status jobs (Brown 1984). Alan Walker's (1982) work has similarly drawn attention to the effect of discrimination against disabled young people, which often leads them to leave school underqualified and to enter lower-grade jobs. Thus, gender, race, ethnicity and disability are all likely to structure transitions through the education system and into the labour market, as well as social class, as studies increasingly recognize.

Stratification in patterns of leaving school creates stratification of other transitions to adulthood. We shall see in Chapter 4 how economic transitions gain pace in the parental home as young people enter employment, and this is affected by class expectations as well as stratification of opportunity. Working-class young people were expected to leave school at the minimum age, starting work, earning a wage and contributing towards the household (Willis, 1977). In contrast, in middle-class families it was more likely to be the case that parents supported and subsidized their children through their extended education, rather than expecting any financial contribution in return. Although there was variation in patterns, there was a normative ideology based on the connection between transitions, so that leaving education was associated with starting work and economic independence (see Wallace, 1988). Those who phased their transitions in non-normative ways were described as having made 'premature' or 'late' transitions. Increasingly, the more recent emphasis has been on describing working-class transitions as premature, rather than middle-class transitions as delayed.

These normative patterns could be fulfilled only in an era of full employment, as we shall explore later, but other changes have occurred which have also disrupted the transition from school to work. Alongside the changes in the labour market, there have been changes in the education system.

THE EXPANSION OF THE EDUCATION SYSTEM

The expansion of the education system since the 1970s has created a new set of transitional phases and new forms of internal stratification have emerged. Education has been associated with certain patterns of

Table 2.1 Expansion of the education system

Higher education	Secondary and Further Education
Increased university provision	Raising of school leaving age
Second tier – polytechnics	Further education colleges
Open University	More vocational qualifications
Access courses	

dependency, and the expansion of educational provision results in new problems for financing the increasing numbers who find themselves in a lengthening 'transition' phase. In the following pages we consider the expansion in different sectors of education and examine its effect on the young people's transitions to adulthood (see Table 2.1).

Higher education

The expansion of higher education serves to extend the dependency of young people on their families or state grants, but also, some have argued, contributes towards increasing individualization. In Britain, some of the most significant changes in their long-term effect occurred as a result of the Robbins Report in 1963. This report explicitly sets out higher education as a basic right of citizenship. The 'Robbins principle', as it became known, claimed that all who had the ability should have the right to higher education, a right which was guaranteed by the parallel provision of maintenance grants. Thus new universities were built, old ones expanded and some colleges of technology gained university status. A second tier of higher education was developed in the 1970s with the creation of polytechnics and a variety of institutions aimed to provide more technological and vocational education. The founding of the Open University in 1972 allowed people to take degrees part-time and this became the largest single higher education institution in terms of recruitment (Halsey, 1988; *Social Trends 18*, 1988). Participation did indeed increase across all social classes, but those who benefited the most were still the middle classes, and university or college became an integral part of the normative middle-class transition pattern. As an illustration of this, Figure 2.2 shows the class composition of students in higher education in 1986, in relation to the class distribution in Britain as a whole.

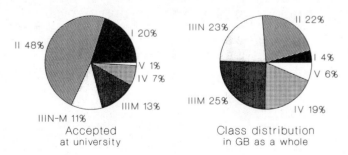

Figure 2.2 University home candidate acceptances by Registra General's social class, 1986

Source: UCCA, cited in Halsey (1988); *1981 Census statistics.*

By the 1960s, higher education was one of the fastest growing national industries (Halsey, 1988): between 1962/63 and 1967/68 the numbers of students grew from 217 000 to 370 000, and by 1980 there were 524 000 in higher education (Layard *et al.*, 1969). The ratio of university entrants to those qualified to go to university increased from 1 in 20 in 1955, to 1 in 10 by 1967 (although it has increased only slightly since then). Following the expansion of first-degree courses came the expansion of provision for second degrees: the numbers taking second degrees rose from 31 900 in 1970 to 33 600 in 1985, reflecting a long-term trend (*Social Trends 18*, 1988). In this way, patterns of transition into the professional and managerial classes were extended.

At the same time, new forms of stratification emerged between different types of degree, and there was inequality of status between institutions. It became important whether a polytechnic or university was attended, and which sort of university it was, as well as what class of degree was obtained. These new ways of differentiating between the increasing numbers of graduates were important in securing jobs and social status. The system generated its own internal stratification.

During the 1980s, despite cuts in government funding, the popularity of higher education has continued. The Government White Paper in 1991, linking central funding of universities more clearly to student numbers, is likely to encourage a dramatic rise in student intake. The expansion of higher education has generated its own demand irrespective of the needs of the labour market. Some of this expansion could come from accepting increasing numbers of school leavers, but some may come from accepting an increasing range and variety of students in different age groups, not just the traditional school leavers. The process of expanding student numbers has offered more opportunities for women to become qualified: the proportion of women in higher education in Britain increased from 41 per cent in 1970 to 47 per cent in 1988 (*Social Trends 21*, 1991). Efforts were made to extend access to higher education, for example, through Access courses which were introduced in the 1980s to help 'non-conventional' students (such as older women, or members of ethnic minorities) to enter the Higher Education sector. Nevertheless many groups remain under-represented.

One consequence of these changes is that the post-war period has seen the construction of an expanding social group of young people in many towns and cities: students. For British students, participation in higher education involves at least three years' commitment. The increasing number of students has significantly affected overall patterns of leaving home, as many British students have to live away from home in order to pursue their studies. The numbers doing so have greatly increased over recent decades: in 1979/80, 81 per cent lived away from home, compared with only 48 per cent in 1920/21 (Halsey, 1988). The shift was made possible by the introduction of maintenance grants in the 1960s and the construction of campus universities. An institutional space was thus created within which student culture and subcultures could flourish. The status of 'student' was recognized, as a period of experimentation and relative personal freedom, away from the immediate influence of the family.

In recent years the position of students as an elite group has been eroded, and the changes in financing arrangements for students, which we shall be discussing in Chapter 3, may result in changing patterns of transition in other areas, including leaving home, and increasing financial responsibilities. From 1964, participation in higher education was based upon maintenance grants paid by local authorities and mandatory for most degrees. These grants were means-tested on parental income. Even so, maintenance grants were continually eroded in the 1970s and 1980s, and the parental contribution gradually rose. The introduction in 1990 of 'top-up loans', to be repaid by the students themselves, represented the beginning of a new era of student finance. More of the costs are now met by parents, employers, or the students themselves, rather than by state grants.

In much of the rest of Western Europe, where degree courses extend for longer than three years and maintenance grants are less comprehensive, it is far more likely that students will continue to live at home. In some parts of Europe and North America, there is a strong part-time labour market in which students work for part of their university and college careers, and thus take longer to complete their degree courses (Ashton and Lowe, 1990). We may see these trends in Britain too as student grants are progressively cut.

Two processes are thus at work: while transitions become less age-related and less structured, with lengthening transitions and widening access, they have at the same time become re-structured around the increasingly recognizable status of 'student'. Some might see this as a new form of stratification, although these processes could also be seen as traditional forms of socialization to the middle class. For example, Bourdieu and Passeron (1977) have described the way in which university education multiplies and enhances what they call 'cultural capital'. Cultural capital, acquired from social background, provides a currency which can be exchanged for jobs, prestige and status. It encompasses the way in which people learn to present themselves, such as the language they use, to gain access to a particular social strata or milieu. These cultural factors are reinforced by the pedagogic style within higher education. Cultural capital is similar to, but not synonymous with economic capital – people may possess one but not the other, although there is usually some correspondence between them. The expansion of the higher education system thus provides the opportunity for the investment of cultural capital by middle-class families, and the creation of reserves of cultural capital by individual students. Bourdieu and Passeron (1977) argue that, rather than widening access, higher education serves to reinforce middle-class cultural codes and extend them to other sections of the population. Higher education provides a style, a 'habitus' which later becomes a reference point and a source of common experience; a degree thus represents not just a qualification but a symbolic resource, and a common culture with other graduates. In this way, education reproduces social classes and status groups.

This monolithic view of 'culture' neglects, however, the variety of forms that culture can take in different educational sectors and amongst different groups of students. Cultures can be actively espoused from the 'bottom up' as well as being imposed from above. Students can develop their own subcultures, including styles and politics, which may or may not be class-related. Alternative ways of understanding this process are discussed in Chapter 6, including the way in which 'cultural capital' can be mobilized by some young people to create an independent role in the consumer markets.

Non-advanced further education

At other levels of the education system, too, new routes were created, with the expansion of the non-advanced further education sector during the 1970s and 1980s. The further education (FE) colleges were originally developed to provide vocational training, but as the numbers of people taking day release from employment declined with the number of apprenticeship places, so the FE colleges shifted towards providing opportunities for other courses (such as General Certificate of Education A and O Level courses) to be taken. In addition, the creation and expansion of various vocational qualifications such as the Business and Technical Education (BTEC) qualifications and other vocational qualifications created a new constituency (Gleeson, 1987). Finally, FE also sometimes provided an 'off-the-job' training element of the Youth Training Scheme (Dale, 1985). Increasing demand for certification meant there was an expanding market for post-school qualification of a non-advanced kind. There was consequently a rise of 174 000 in the numbers of FE students between 1981 and 1986 (*Social Trends 19*, 1989), and for some of these, going to college was an alternative to becoming unemployed.

The overall consequence, as with higher education, is an increase in the variety of courses at FE level, increasing differentiation between courses at different levels, and further stratification amongst students. The extension of education and training to wider groups means that more young people remain dependent on their families or the state for longer periods. Some FE students are able to obtain maintenance grants, but many must pay their own fees and rely on financial support from their families or from employers (or finance themselves from part-time work) in order to continue their education in this way.

Thus, the expansion of the higher and further education sectors means that the status of student has become more universally recognized. As numbers have increased, so there is increasing internal differentiation in the kinds of students, kinds of courses and degree of financial support they receive from the state. The expansion of 'studenthood' as an intermediate status as of right allows for a period of 'unfixed' identity and personal experimentation, for *some* students. This has generated the circumstances under which new social movements – animal rights, Green politics, the women's movement, and so on – have been able to flourish. This transitional status, removed from the traditional constraints of the labour market, encourages political and personal identifications which are not explicitly class-based.

THE CHANGING LABOUR MARKET

Alongside changes in the educational system there have been major changes in the structures of industry and employment. The structure of transition from education into the labour market therefore needs to be seen more generally in the context of the restructuring of capitalism over the latter part of the twentieth century. The normative model of the transition from school to the labour market was premised on conditions of full employment and the traditional large-scale industrial and bureaucratic organizations which existed in the early post-war era. Centralized structures, with spatially concentrated workforces, constructed the transition into work for different social classes. The industrial cities were often the locations in which large national industries were located and this form of work organization was often associated with urbanization. This phase of capitalism was likewise associated with large, corporatist trades unions organized at a national level to protect the interests of workers (Lash and Urry, 1987).

These features were encouraged and underpinned by Keynesian demand-management intervention in the economy. The expansion of the welfare state in the post-war era was undertaken on the same nationalized, centralized, planned model, conceived to provide support for people through all phases of their lives. The *right* to work was thus an essential part of the post-war model of citizenship and *access* to work was to be guaranteed by an expanding labour market in a planned economy. The education system was a crucial part of the planned economy, helping to stratify school leavers according to levels corresponding with the different levels of the occupational class structure, and socializing them through the bureaucratic criteria of formal examinations. The growth of the service sector in the labour market since the 1950s produced a demand for white collar and professional jobs and thus structural opportunities for upward social mobility, mainly for men with qualifications, but also increasingly for women (Halsey *et al.*, 1980; Abbott and Wallace, 1990). The right to work and to education came to be seen as integral to social citizenship for women as well as men (although the legal right to enter employment in a free labour market is recognized as an aspect of civil citizenship).

In the 1970s major changes began to take place. First, unemployment rose steeply and British industry started to be restructured. Much of the traditional manufacturing sector closed down as multinational corporations moved their manufacturing operations overseas. National organizations were increasingly replaced by transnational organizations, which were able to separate production from management, and link geographically separated divisions through telecommunications networks. Large-scale organization started to be replaced by small-scale organization, 'flexible specialization', subcontracted work and 'consultancies' (Bagguley, 1991). Temporary and performance-related contract work began to replace regular life-time employment, and an example of this can be seen in the restructuring of the steel industry in South Wales (Fevre, 1987). The expectation of full-time employment was replaced by an acceptance of unemployment, part-time work, home working or temporary work (Lash and Urry, 1987). The demise of large-scale traditional industries also resulted in the collapse of the apprenticeship training system by the mid-1980s (Roberts, 1984). The trades unions, weakened by unemployment and the increase in casual work, were unable to resist the removal of employment protection from workers. The principle of the right to work was increasingly challenged.

These trends were encouraged by the election in 1979 of a Conservative Government which had pledged to cut public expenditure and de-regulate the labour market. The Government claimed to reduce the role of the state in regulating social life and pull back from the 'paternalistic' state intervention which had been taken for granted under the Keynesian consensus. Policies for encouraging private ownership of housing, transport, education and health were introduced along with the privatization of public utilities. State services were cut back and sub-contracted to the private sector, in an attempt to cut costs and to 'roll back the frontiers of the state'. In this context, citizenship was defined by the Conservative Government as the right to choose between services.

These patterns of flexibility in employment may have the effect of introducing new demands on the education system. The ideal of mass education, constructed around the need to reproduce a workforce organized along 'Fordist' principles, and around large bureaucratic structures, would need instead to educate for flexibility and change (Brown and Lauder, 1992). Traditional education was indeed criticized by the Right for being too traditional and inflexible and instead the 'spirit of enterprise' was ideologically encouraged by a government influenced by 'New Right' thinking. Schemes such as 'Enterprise Allowance' and 'Enterprise in Higher Education' encouraged young people to use their initiatives and even become self-employed. A study by MacDonald and Coffield (1991) of 'young entrepreneurs' indicates that some at least were inspired by this ethic.

These trends should not be exaggerated, however. The devolution of the organizational structures of large firms co-exists with an increasing concentration of capital in multi-national units. This has been encouraged by financial de-regulation by several major Western governments with 'neo-liberal' parties in power. In Britain this could be seen as a return to an unregulated *laissez-faire* model of the labour market. In the small-scale enterprise sector and rural areas there had always been a great deal of flexibility, non-regulation and uncertainty (Wallace *et al.*, 1991a). The rising number of business start-ups has been matched by a spectacular number of business failures and the work of MacDonald and Coffield (1991) indicates that the success of local enterprise is always dependent upon the strength of the local economy. Furthermore, the continuity and regularity in employment careers for young entrants to the labour market in the past can also be exaggerated: there was often flexibility at an individual level and evidence suggests that a common pattern among young people was to change jobs frequently for at least a few years (Baxter, 1975; Carter, 1975; Cherry, 1976). The main changes in the situation of young people in the labour market can be summarized thus:

- Abolition of Wages Councils
- Withdrawal of employment protection
- Increase in youth unemployment
- Reduction in youth wages
- Loss of apprenticeships
- Increase in part-time and casual working
- Introduction of training schemes.

The introduction of structured flexibility in the labour market has often been at the expense of marginal members of the workforce such as women, young people, disabled workers and those from ethnic minorities. 'Flexibility' means the possibility of laying people off, paying them low wages or introducing short time and wage cuts. The risk and uncertainty is borne by individual young people as well as employers, as secure employment becomes less and less common. Developments in the labour market have thus led to the de-regulation of transition patterns and work careers, as regular employment has been replaced by temporary, self-employed and flexible work. This has made planned transitions more difficult (Myles, 1991).

In these circumstances, the right to a full-time job as a basic right of citizenship was more difficult to demand, let alone achieve. The new emphasis on the market after 1980 was incompatible with Marshall's notion of universal citizenship; the market is bound to generate unequal access to jobs, and cannot provide guaranteed employment.

Youth wages and conditions of work

Those young people who were able to go straight into employment in the 1980s were not as well off as their counterparts in the 1960s had been. The introduction of schemes such as the Young Workers Scheme followed by the New Workers Scheme in the 1980s had been intended to lower young people's wages so that they could 'price themselves back into work' in the terminology of monetarist economists. These schemes subsidized only those employers who paid low wages. This was coupled with the abolition of Wages Council protection which had covered some low-paid jobs done by young people. In addition the weakening of the Trades Union movement through unemployment and defeats in a series of strikes over the 1980s (resulting in a fall in membership from around half the workforce to around a third) meant that unions were not in a good position to protect young people's wages or conditions of work or to oppose the substitution of an expensive older worker by a cheaper younger one.

Data derived from the *New Earnings Surveys* 1970 to 1990 (Figure 2.3) show that whereas young people's wages had risen as a proportion of adult wages during the 1970s, they had dropped again in the 1980s. There is a far smaller income disparity between girls' and adult female wages than between boys' and adult male wages; this is only because of the low level of adult women's wages, in comparison with that of adult men, compared with a somewhat greater parity of wages between young men and young women. In fact, even within the group of young wage earners the 16–19 Initiative found huge variations in youth wages (Roberts *et al.*, 1991). Fewer young people are in work, and more are getting training allowances rather than wages. Those in work have little power to bargain for higher pay. The decline in the working conditions

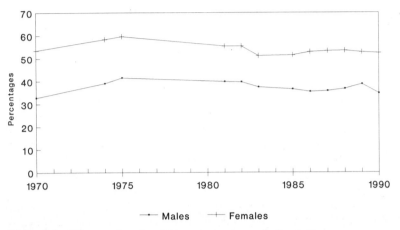

Figure 2.3   Wages of under-18s as percentage of all-adult wages
Source: New Earnings Surveys.

of young people is partly a consequence of the fact that they have no
collective voice and their interests are easily ignored.

The rise in unemployment

The most dramatic change in the 1970s was the rise in unemployment. The oil crisis of the early 1970s depressed the already flagging
British industry and resulted in a cutback in employment and in
recruitment to jobs (Roberts, 1984). The unemployment rate for
adults rose from 3 per cent in 1961 to 6 per cent in 1976 and stood at
14 per cent in 1988 (Halsey, 1988) despite the many revisions in the
methods of counting, generally designed to keep unemployment figures down. Studies at the time indicated that young people were
particularly severely affected by the rise in general levels of unemployment in a 'pendulum effect', which was an amplified version of that
affecting adults (Makeham, 1980; Raffe, 1987). In the 1970s it was
increasingly argued that young people were now structurally disadvantaged in the labour market in a manner which had not been seen
before (even during the Great Depression). The rise in unemployment
undermined the right to work as a basic tenet of citizenship. Young
people were seen as having less of a right to work than other groups,
as well as having less of a right to a full wage.

Unemployment exacerbated other forms of disadvantage. Within
the overall trend, school leavers with no qualifications were most
likely to find themselves unemployed (Holland Report, 1977), and

black school leavers were twice as likely to be out of work as white school leavers (Cross, 1987; Cross and Smith, 1987; Wrench *et al.*, 1989). Disabled school leavers were likewise a particularly disadvantaged group (Walker, 1982). Young women, however, found it easier to find jobs in some places than did young men (Wallace, 1987a). Unemployed young people were thrown back upon their household resources. The phenomenon of an unemployed son or daughter was a new situation for many families to deal with, but those which were most likely to have an unemployed young person at home, were often also the least financially equipped to cope. A study by Joan Payne (1987) found that unemployed young people were likely to live in households where other members were also unemployed. Furthermore, they were more likely to live in poorer households (Roll, 1990). Unemployment was also unevenly distributed across regions – those with declining industries were especially hard hit (Massey and Meagan, 1982), and patterns of transition from school to work varied considerably across different labour markets (Ashton *et al.*, 1987; Roberts *et al.*, 1991). During the mid-1980s, the economy picked up again and opportunities for young labour market entrants expanded, particularly in the South East of England. Then in 1990, another recession struck and the areas which had most expanded in the 1980s were particularly severely hit: this recession thus particularly affected service industries in the South East.

The consequence of these waves of recession has been to make it common for young people to be unemployed for at least part of their post-school careers. Those worst affected were the lowest qualified, the group who had previously gone directly into low-skilled jobs on leaving school. The families they came from are the ones which would expect them to be bringing in a wage and contributing towards household resources. Instead they were unemployed and claiming social security, but as Chapter 3 shows, many of their social security entitlements have been withdrawn and they are now even more likely to be a financial burden on their families.

Studies by social psychologists indicate that unemployment causes depression and a loss of self-confidence, although the 'normality' of unemployment for this age group means that they are able to redefine themselves and their use of time and resources (Kelvin and Jarret, 1985; Wallace, 1987a). Whilst studies of 'the unemployed' have emphasized their homogeneity, it is evident that there are different kinds of unemployed young people with different experiences. Thus, they could be unemployed between jobs, or after leaving school, training, college or university. Unemployment could have very different meanings in these different contexts. In a previous empirical study, Wallace (1987a) found that rather than classifying young people as either employed or unemployed it was more helpful to look at their 'employment careers', and to see how different periods of unemployment were phased and for how long a person was unemployed after leaving school and in subsequent years. Some were unemployed only occasionally and others for long periods. It is these *biographical* experiences of unemployment rather than cross-sectional counts which help us understand the implications of unemployment for different groups of school leavers. Experiences of unemployment are also likely to have a profound effect on other life-course transitions such as leaving home and family formation. Those without the money or employment status have to effect these transitions differently or not at all.

The extension of training

Holland (1977) and others have suggested that young people's disadvantages in the labour market were caused by their lack of training: they were unemployed because they were not equipped for work. This analysis suggested that workers with different and more flexible skills would be needed in the future; furthermore, traditional training for apprenticeships was no longer appropriate as demand for the kinds of 'masculine skills' in traditional industrial sectors had decreased. Myles (1991) suggests that we can see this as a transition from a 'Fordist' life course – where a person was trained for a life-time job – to one where there was constant change and flexibility in employment conditions. It was argued that what was needed was training for flexibility. The Manpower Service Commission (MSC), originally set up in the early 1970s, was expanded to take on the job of youth training as a solution to this labour market mis-match. The Youth Opportunities Programme (YOP) was introduced in 1978 as a result. It provided temporary, six-month training periods for those out of work in an attempt to equip them for the job market, but also with the aim of maintaining some controls over young people.

These temporary schemes were replaced in 1983 by the Youth Training Scheme (YTS): the most significant intervention in the transition from school to work to date. Designed as a one-year, permanent bridge between school and work for all school leavers, it was a 'great step forward' from the Youth Opportunities Programme. Modelled to some extent upon the 'dual system' in Germany (see Wallace, 1991b), it was intended to introduce a universal training system into Britain for the first time (Finn, 1987; Ainley and Corney, 1990; Wallace and Cross, 1990). Given the long-standing reluctance of employers to invest in training, it was funded by massive investment from government so that by the mid-1980s the MSC controlled a budget of £2000 million and employed over a million people in various capacities (Ainley and Corney, 1990). Young people were able to undertake a number of different types of training in an internally-differentiated system. The YTS was extended to two years in 1986. It represented a solution because it provided apparently worthwhile activity for young people at a time when the demographic increase in the numbers of young people coincided with rising youth unemployment. The intention was to introduce a universal status of 'trainee' or 'student' for all people under the age of 18 years, rather than to see them as 'workers' or 'unemployed'. Although never as universal as had been hoped, this did in practice introduce a new stage in the transition into work.

As a result of these changes, a right to training was introduced for 16- and 17-year-olds; a guaranteed place would be provided for everyone who wanted training, and this in many ways replaced their right to work. Market principles were later introduced into training provision, with the introduction of 'training vouchers' which could be cashed in by consumers of training. This can be interpreted as a redefinition of social citizenship rights in terms of market principles.

From the end of the 1980s however, the large birth cohort was already working its way through the age group and it was projected that there would be a fall in the supply of school leavers by the 1990s. There was also a rise in the demand for school leavers in labour markets such as in the South East where the economy was expanding once more. Employers in areas like Swindon could afford to ignore the youth training schemes and offered school leavers attractive packages to leave school straightaway, before gaining additional qualifications – at least until the recent recession hit this area; in the more depressed areas such as Liverpool, however, the schemes retained their importance (see Roberts and Parsell, 1988, Roberts *et al.*, 1989).

Having been expanded in the 1980s, the YTS was de-constructed again and renamed Youth Training (YT) in 1990. At this time it was organizationally linked to adult Employment Training (ET) and under this latter scheme 'trainees' worked for a small allowance in addition to their social security. They were 'encouraged' to join such schemes by the threat of having their social security entitlement withdrawn if they refused. Until this point the trades unions had supported the youth training schemes, but now they withdrew their support from the Manpower Services Commission. At this time, its budget was cut and it was replaced, first by the Training Commission, and then by the Training Agency, whose responsibilities were devolved to local employer-led Training and Enterprise Councils. The Training Commission has in the early 1990s been further dismantled and absorbed into the Department of Employment in England and Wales and renamed once more as the Training, Education and Enterprise Department. In Scotland it became part of Scottish Enterprise. Amongst all these organizational changes, the Government's commitment to training decreased in the light of falling unemployment and increased regional differentiation in the nature and quality of schemes (Chandler and Wallace, 1990). Instead of the regulated and centralized training scheme which had been envisaged in the early 1980s, the schemes actually contributed to the development of decentralized and unregulated work patterns by encouraging temporary employment.

These training schemes mean that many young people have a mediated relationship to the labour market and to production, and are 'suspended' in a 'surrogate labour market' (Lee, 1990; Lee *et al.*, 1990). This 'surrogate labour market' is itself internally differentiated in a number of ways: for example, there are distinctions between different kinds of scheme (employer-based, workshop-based) and between different types of training (for skilled, semi-skilled or unskilled manual work). Schemes were highly variable: some trainees were used by employers as cheap substitutes for regular workers and were dismissed at the end of their training, but in other cases, schemes were used as the basis of firm training and recruitment into jobs.

Within the YTS, schemes are sex-differentiated. An ethnographic study by Bates (1989a) found that girls who undertook schemes in design were highly motivated because they wrongly imagined that the scheme would lead to a glamorous career. Girls on a 'Care' scheme on the other hand developed an occupational culture which helped them to withstand the emotional pressures and hard physical work of working with elderly people. There was a continuity between their home and their training environments in terms of the heavy domestic labour expected of them in both spheres (Bates, 1989b). Young men undertaking a chef's course were enthusiastic and motivated in their orientation to the scheme whilst those undertaking training leading to unskilled work were subversive and resistant (Riseborough 1991). Hence, although the schemes form a 'surrogate labour market' they create their own forms of stratification between and within genders.

Trainees are not, according to some studies, being socialized into 'real' jobs on many of the schemes: some trainees are shocked or disappointed when they experience 'real' work which is not what they had been led to expect. Others have suggested, by contrast, that these surrogate schemes socialize young people into the low-skilled work, low pay and low positions which they should expect in the 1990s labour market (Buswell, 1986; White, 1990). The evidence suggests that about one-third of trainees do not find jobs when the schemes end. Furthermore, it has been argued that their training is geared more towards internal labour markets than external ones – that is, they are trained for a particular job in a particular firm rather than for a transferable skill (Raffe, 1991a). This has in turn fuelled the apparent need for certification at all levels of the labour market – although the rating employers give to YTS certificates was uncertain. More recently, the YTS certificate has been abolished: instead YT trainees work towards other sorts of qualifications. Although intended as the 'training solution' there is a great deal of cynicism about the schemes from both employers and trainees. One feature of Youth Training is that it undergoes radical reorganization from year to year and hence has an air of deliberate transience.

The introduction of Youth Training therefore serves to mediate the relationship between young people and the labour market. Instead of entering work and work cultures directly, they have an indirect experience of work through the schemes. Home environment and work destinations still structure the process and help to shape young people's experiences within it, but they are also subject to the influence of what happens within the scheme. The low level of training allowances makes young people who may have been traditionally earning a wage at this age, more dependent upon parental support. These allowances take no account of young people who may want to leave home or of their costs of living. The Youth Training Schemes, by not being classified as 'employment', avoid much of the Equal Opportunities legislation and employment protection legislation. Trainee allowances are currently £29.50 per week in the first year, rising to £35 in the second year. Overall, though, the amounts have not kept pace with inflation and in real terms are now lower than when the schemes were first introduced.

In 1988, the role of Youth Training was reinforced when young people under 18 years of age lost their entitlement to unemployment benefit on the basis that they would be offered a training place. This linking of employment and Youth Training, and the subsequent penalizing of ET and YT participants who did not accept places on schemes, represented a further shift in the concept of citizenship consistent with 'New Right' philosophy. Access to welfare rights was based not on membership of society but upon the responsibility to work and to contribute. The responsibility of 'able-bodied' claimants of unemployment benefit to join schemes instead is just one aspect of this attempt to reinforce the moral basis of citizenship based upon obligations. This was spelled out by Mead (1986: 143) in the USA: 'Only when work obligation seems as certain as "death and taxation" will non-work be overcome'. It is a philosophy which sees the poor as being responsible for their own poverty.

The changes in young people's entitlement to welfare (discussed more fully in Chapter 3) have reinforced the tendency towards flexibility in the labour market, by providing a ready workforce which is familiar with perpetual change and which does not expect continuous employment careers.

Part-time work

Whilst the importance of full-time work has declined for those under 21 years, the importance of part-time work has increased. Once again, we can see the effect of increasingly flexible employment practices on young people's transitions. With increasing dependence upon state benefits and parents, part-time work offers some opportunity for economic independence. It can take a range of different forms for young people both before and after the school leaving age: it can mean a regular Saturday, evening or morning job, one-off casual jobs, holiday jobs or work which is done 'informally' for friends and neighbours. These jobs are also undertaken whilst young people are on Youth Training schemes, whilst they are at college or university and whilst they have a full-time job (see Howieson, 1990; Hutson and Cheung, 1991).

Analysis of the Labour Force Survey by Angela Dale (1988), found that though very few young people aged 16–19 years were working part-time for their main job in the absence of anything else, this figure had gone up from 5 per cent to 6 per cent between 1979 and 1984. Part-time working was, however, important not as a substitute for full-time jobs but as a way of supplementing low incomes in the context of young people's otherwise marginal economic situations: it was a way of supplementing grants, Youth Training Scheme allowances or of gaining an income whilst at school. Studies suggest that the practice of part-time working in youth is more common among the working class than among the middle class (Finn, 1987), and among women more than among men (Griffin, 1985), although with the decline in student support we may see students increasingly involved. In her study of the Isle of Sheppey in the late 1970s and early 1980s, Wallace (1987a) found that all young people in a working-class community had undertaken casual jobs at some point. In her later study of young people in rural areas, she found that young people made important and sometimes substantial contributions to family enterprises and farms whilst working as YTS trainees or students (Wallace *et al.*, 1990). If we add to this the informal services that young people of this age group provide, such as baby-sitting, we can see that there is a large unrecorded area of 'economic activity' in which young people are engaged (discussed further in Chapter 4).

These economic activities may provide important sources of income for those who are not in formal employment.

Part-time work can have an important effect on the economic circumstances of young people in transitional statuses between school and the labour market; thus, for example, Roberts *et al.* (1991) found that students with part-time work were often better off than workers with full-time jobs. It seems likely that part-time working is a growing sector of the labour market, among students whose vacation entitlement to benefits has been withdrawn, among trainees on low allowances, or among workers with full-time but low-paid jobs.

THE 'YOUTH DEBATE' OF THE 1980S

Within the sociology of youth in Britain, the debate which has dominated the 1980s has been limited to discussion about the extent to which transition into the labour market is structured, and the extent to which there is freedom of choice. There is general agreement that pathways out of school are still structured by factors such as social class, family background, academic achievement (particularly in traditional academic rather than vocational subjects) and opportunities in the local labour market. The debate is about the extent of predeterminism, rather than whether it exists (see Raffe, 1991b). Roberts has identified a number of transition paths: the academic route, the vocational education route; the route from Youth Training to jobs and the route directly into jobs. Some school leavers do not fit this pattern, having no identifiable career. Roberts later modified his position to define only two clear trajectories – the academic route and skilled manual training; the rest had no obvious trajectory (see Roberts and Parsell, 1990). Raffe (1991b) has contested this conclusion, arguing that the fortunes of new workers depend upon the labour market context in which they find themselves, rather than upon their trajectories out of school.

A related element of the 'youth debate' has been about 'choice'. Roberts (1968), arguing against the social psychologists Ginzberg *et al.* (1951) and Super (1953), pointed out that young people's destinations were determined by labour market structures and any idea of 'choice' was merely an illusion. He still holds this view (see Roberts and Parsell, 1990). Raffe, on the other hand, has indicated that opting for a low status career can be a rational 'choice' for young people, given the constraints within which they live (Raffe, 1991b). The concept of individualization has now addressed the issue, and according to this thesis, 'choice' is not free, but is forced upon young people by the changing structures within which they find themselves; young people are made to choose between sometimes limited alternatives and construct, in the process, their self-identities. In a previous paper we have argued (see Jones and Wallace, 1990) that young people are so constrained by the structures of education, employment and training, that they have less choice than in previous decades when there were more jobs. At one time the 'choice', within constraints, was between education and employment – but also between different forms of employment. Now the choice has apparently widened and is between education, training and employment, but the constraints appear also to have increased – there is very little choice in terms of forms of employment, and young people tend to be channelled into training schemes rather than choosing between them. The whole debate needs, however, to be located in terms of other aspects of young people's biographies.

DEPENDENCY AND CONTROL

How far are young people able to acquire freedom and independence within these changes? The Youth Training scheme was introduced in the wake of violent inner-city confrontations with the police in 1981 and 1985 (and again in 1991). The media-created spectre of unemployed, alienated young men threatening the social order was a powerful image in the 1970s and early 1980s. There were demands for social control and a political emphasis on law and order.

The status of 'pupil', 'student' or 'trainee' is a subordinate one, involving supervision and control by others in authority. Pupils, students and trainees are required to conform to particular models of behaviour introduced by the organization to which they are attached and their behaviour is subject to scrutiny and examination by those in control. The financial stringency under which trainees and students must live is another form of subordination and control. Some studies of youth training schemes have argued that one of the aims of the programme was to produce conformity (Moos, 1983; Buswell, 1986), through training in work disciplines, such as punctuality, self-presentation and compliance, as much as to impart skills.

Although Youth Training may have been intended to produce conformity, in practice young people are able to resist such pressures and assert some autonomy within the training context. Hence, Parsons (1991) found that in YTS classroom sessions, trainees preferred to discuss sex rather than the official curriculum, and thus undermined the legitimacy of the pedagogic mode. Teachers complied with this in order to maintain some degree of authority. Riseborough's (1991) study of 'lads' on a low status scheme and Bates's (1989b) study of girls on 'Care' schemes both found that trainees resisted their scheme and undermined its legitimacy. However, in more high status schemes studied by both these authors, the ideologies and aims of YTS were absorbed by trainees, although they still manipulated the situation in their own ways.

These studies suggest that, while young people are subordinated by their new social roles, they are still able to develop their own spheres of autonomy and independence. Indeed the 'surrogate labour market' may offer new opportunities to experiment with identities and options. We have indicated that in the days of fuller employment, job-changing performed a similar function for young people experimenting with their labour market identities. Where autonomy and independence can only be achieved through resistance to the system, rather than through working within the system, then the obligations of citizenship are not being fulfilled. It is however unrealistic to expect that young people will take on the responsibilities of citizenship in circumstances where their citizenship rights – in this case perhaps to a degree of choice in the labour market, perhaps to an adequate wage – are not acknowledged.

STRUCTURING DEPENDENCY AND CITIZENSHIP

The traditional concept of an orderly transition was more applicable in the 1950s and 1960s, and transitions have become more disordered since. Indeed the Youth Training Scheme was an attempt to impose some order on an apparently disordered and unregulated youth labour market, though it has only been partly successful. New pathways of transition and new forms of differentiation have emerged. There is more uncertainty in embarking upon post-school careers. This has led Olk (1988) to argue that in Germany the youth phase has become 'destandardized'. Structures such as training and education that used to be associated with adolescence can now extend into adulthood (and indeed do in many countries); nor is there a single one-way path of transition – young people can move back and forth between these different states. This stance tends to exaggerate the orderliness of transitions in the past. However, all the extensive studies of the 1980s agree that there is now more likely to be an indirect entry into work, rather than a direct entry from school. Young people have an extended junior status before they become full adult workers. Rather than going from school to work, they may pass through a number of transitional phases first. Their transition to economic independence is thus extended, and we shall see in Chapter 3 the extent to which youth is increasingly becoming a period of confusion, characterized by half-dependence and half-independence.

The expansion of education, the creation of transitional institutions for young people and the disorganization of the phases of transition are all also associated with increasing differentiation between young people. Although trainees, students and the unemployed may all be in transitional statuses, they are not equal groups, and they have very different long-term trajectories. For students, a period of subordination and relative poverty in youth may precede getting a higher paid job and high status in society as an adult, whereas for trainees and those who are unemployed it could become part of a lifetime pattern of second-class citizenship. We have briefly discussed the relevance of 'cultural capital' in the student case. In the case of students, their reserves of cultural capital, their greater likelihood of extended financial support from their parents, their involvement in the political arena, and their relatively good prospects for the future, may all provide them with some degree of power in youth. Trainees and young people in the labour market are in comparison relatively defenceless in the face of government policies which can reduce their employment protection, their wages, and their chances of full participation in society.

3

SOCIAL CITIZENSHIP

BY PROXY?

While the education system and labour market structure economic status in youth, and thence access to the rights of citizenship, it is through the social security system that the social allocation of citizenship is determined, principally for those who are unable to achieve economic independence through employment. Many of the changes in education and the labour market which we have discussed in Chapter 2 have led either to a loss or to a reduction of income for young people. They have resulted in increasing dependency on families, and have re-defined the role of families in relation to dependence upon state benefits. In this chapter we will be examining in more detail changes in the way the state benefit system has recognized the position of young people over time. Then, with particular reference to social security, National Insurance, student grants and housing benefits, we shall consider the implications of recent changes for the way in which young people can begin to participate in society as citizens.

Social citizenship, as reflected in the social security system, is based on assumptions about young people's status and their family relationships. These assumptions therefore have implications for the ways in which young people and their families are able to live. It is assumed that children can derive their citizenship rights through their parents, by proxy as it were; when they become adult, they can be citizens in their own right. We need to question these assumptions on a number of levels. Specifically, are rights in practice indirectly transmitted in the way suggested from parent to child, and secondly, how are we to know when a young person should be entitled instead to direct access to the rights of social citizenship? In this context, we need to ask whether payment of welfare benefits should be made to young people directly or to parents on their behalf? If paid to young people, can it be assumed that they will pass on to their parents the cost of their keep? If given to parents, can it be assumed that any money will be distributed back to young people to enable them to invest in their futures and develop independence? Furthermore, can it be assumed that young people have families who are in a position to help them either by providing a home or with money?

The balance between paying or not paying benefits, and between paying direct to young people or paying to mother, father or other guardian on their behalf, has shifted as policies have changed in recent years. The policies are based on implicit assumptions about internal household dynamics, including parent–child economic transfers. Policy-making has been based on ignorance of issues such as how much board money young people pay their parents (and who pays) or how much pocket money children receive (and who receives it). The household has been deemed instead a 'private sphere' within which people must negotiate their own relationships and so the concepts of dependence and independence have remained unchallenged (Jones 1991a). We shall be examining the economic relationship between young people and their parents, and the transitions to economic independence which are enacted within the 'private sphere' of family life, in Chapter 4.

Although the relationship between parents and young people has been subject to continual re-definition within the social security system over the last century, at no period was it intended to provide young people with the wherewithal to make independent transitions to adulthood, such as transitions out of the parental home. The gradual and partial recognition of the needs of young people was framed by their position of dependence within their families and the costs to their parents of keeping them there. However, it was often the case that combinations of different benefits, such as social security, housing benefits and student maintenance grants, were used by young people as ways of leaving the parental home and achieving independence from parents, and from the 1960s these became increasingly important in this respect. The payment of benefits to young people directly rather than to their parents on their behalf was beginning to allow this possibility and it is this shift (and subsequent swing back to older practices) which we shall now document in more detail. At the same time, the history of social security provision has shown an increasing tendency to be based on standardized transitions to adulthood, so that benefits and access to them have become increasingly age-graded, and less responsive to individual need. In these terms, rights to social citizenship have become increasingly age-structured, and access more limited.

THE HISTORY OF SOCIAL SECURITY FOR YOUNG PEOPLE

The history of social security has been divided into three phases reflecting shifts in the climate of policy-making (Harris, 1989):

- 1900–1946 Development of National Insurance
- 1946–1979 The 'universal' welfare state
- 1979–1991 The return to *laissez-faire.*

The period 1900–1946 is characterized by a state increasingly, but reluctantly, involved in the provision of very basic benefits in the context of the Poor Law; the period 1946–1979 was one in which the 'universal' welfare state was established in Britain and benefits were paid to a widening range of people for an increasing number of reasons; the period after 1979 was one of conscious retrenchment and selective targeting of welfare services. The policies of the latter period, deriving from what has been termed 'New Right' political philosophy, have aimed to return young people to being the responsibility of their families, mostly for reasons of cutting cost rather than moral reform (see Chapter 4, and Abbott and Wallace, 1991). By considering the history of social security more generally, we can trace the shifting assumptions around young people's dependence and independence, and see how state policies have structured access to social citizenship rights in youth.

1900–1946: The development of National Insurance

The period in which the early foundations of the welfare state were laid was one in which the state became reluctantly more and more interventionist. The family was seen as a 'private sphere' with children 'hidden' in it, within the Victorian legal and economic system. Both the administration of the Poor Law and the work of the Charity Organization Society in the nineteenth century were concerned with administering relief on the basis of 'deserving' cases and in return for evidence of moral improvement. This represented a form of 'policing' of poor families, according to Donzelot (1979). From the early origins of the Poor Law and state welfare provision, the emphasis was always upon encouraging families to become self-sufficient and to support themselves. The role of charity and parish relief was not to undermine but to encourage this role, commensurate with the dominant *laissez-faire* economic philosophy of Victorian England. Consequently, although the special and separate status of children had been specifically recognized in the Factory Acts of 1833 and the Youthful Offenders Acts of 1854, the state did not accept responsibility for their financial maintenance. The aim was to get the family heads to support their 'dependants' instead.

Nevertheless, many reforms – such as the introduction of universal education at the end of the nineteenth century and the creation of health visiting at the beginning of the twentieth century – impinged irrevocably on the construction of family life and particularly upon the relationship between parents and children (Abbott and Sapsford, 1990). They served to re-define and re-construct parent–child relations.

A move away from the Poor Law system, with its locally provided 'outdoor relief' and workhouses for the destitute, began in the first decades of the twentieth century. The first of these reforms, the Old Age Pensions Act was introduced in 1908 and was followed by the National Insurance Act of 1911 which insured many (but not all) workers against unemployment, old age and ill health if they were between 16 and 70 years of age. There was no allowance for dependants and young people were not specifically recognized unless they were workers. National Insurance eligibility was based upon contributions begun at age 16 – although the age of starting work was at that time 13 (Ogus, 1982). Young workers aged between 13 and 16 were therefore in an anomalous position – not fully recognized either as insured workers or as dependants.

Under the National Insurance system, workers in some industries, their employers and the state would all contribute a share towards an insurance fund, on which those who later had specified needs could claim. Since the system was not universal, it existed alongside the Poor Law and the workhouses which catered for people in circumstances which were not covered by National Insurance. It was only the contributors to National Insurance who benefited: they were expected to make their own provision for dependants. The system was based upon a model of the male adult breadwinner in regular full-time employment as the typical worker.

National Insurance did not in practice protect the majority of young workers since many were engaged in the kinds of casual work which were not subject to National Insurance contributions. A frequent problem at the time was that of 'blind alley' employment whereby young males were employed cheaply until the age of 16 or 18 when they became eligible for higher wages and liable for National Insurance contributions; at this point they were dismissed and replaced by a younger worker. The introduction of National Insurance actually decreased the incentives to employ young people over 16 years. This situation continued after the First World War (when the age of leaving school was raised to 14) and into the inter-war period (when youth unemployment was not considered a problem, since it was apparently older workers who were more likely to suffer unemployment in the Great Depression of the 1930s). Although unemployment may have increased for young people, most were not registered unemployed at the Labour Exchanges and hence their numbers are greatly underestimated. It seems, nevertheless, that having peaked in 1932, youth unemployment levelled off at about 5 per cent, compared with 12 per cent for adults (Rees, and Rees 1982). The National Insurance Scheme precluded those aged under 17 from claiming benefits for which they had been contributing, and even at 17 years gave them only about half the adult rate. Under these circumstances it is hardly surprising that most young people did not even register as unemployed.

What could parents claim for young people? After the First World War, servicemen received an 'out of work' allowance which included an amount for dependants, but it was only in 1921 that the Unemployed Workers (Dependants) Act made temporary provision for dependants in the form of 'winter relief': this was later made permanent in the Unemployment Insurance Act of 1922 (Ogus, 1982). A dependence allowance of one shilling for each child aged between 14 and 16 was introduced, followed by a rise to two shillings in 1934 and to three shillings in 1935 (Harris, 1989). Single persons, young persons aged 14 to 16 and married women were still explicitly excluded from claiming themselves, since they were deemed to be the responsibility of the male breadwinner – although in 1925 the Widows and Orphans Act made provision for those, including young dependants, who had lost their main breadwinner.

The economic climate of the inter-war period created various financial crises for the governments of the day and National Insurance funds were soon gobbled up by rising unemployment and lengthening periods out of work. One government response was to cut benefits. The first people to lose benefits were young workers in 1925, with adults following later. In 1931 the eligibility criteria were tightened up and claimants were required to have worked 30 weeks in the previous two years in order to qualify. Furthermore, young people up to the age of 18 were not to be given 'dole' unconditionally, but instead their benefits were to be tied to participation in training schemes and 'Juvenile Instruction Centres'. Then, as now, it was felt that the young unemployed should be treated differently from adults. Earlier ambiguities were however retained: from 1930 the age for entry into the National Insurance Scheme was reduced to 15 and it was expected that the school leaving age would be raised to 15 to correspond with it; in fact it was not until 1944 that this happened, so the gap between leaving school and eligibility for benefits remained.

Despite the gradual extension of state-administered benefits of various kinds, it was still believed that 'the family' – in the form of the male 'breadwinner' – should support its members from its own efforts. In the 1930s the household income was defined in such a way as to take into account the individual incomes of all household members on the assumption that these were pooled. Eligibility for assistance was determined by the 'household means test' administered by the Public Assistance Committees and later by the Unemployment Assistance Board. The wages of a young employed person living at home were deducted from the parent's unemployment benefit. This affected a large number of people – one-third of households receiving benefit had their income reduced in 1938 for this reason. The household means test was bitterly resented at the time probably because in practice household income was frequently not pooled and young people still expected to retain some income for themselves. The unanticipated consequence of this legislation was that employed young people were encouraged to leave home so that their parents could claim a higher rate of benefit (Finch, 1989).

From 1934, the age of entry to the National Insurance scheme was further reduced to 14 – although no claims could be made until the age of 16. By this time, however, parents were entitled to a dependency addition to their own unemployment benefit. (Girls were entitled to lower rates of benefit than boys, reflecting their lower incomes and the view that they were only temporarily in the labour market before marriage.) Thus, by the Second World War, when unemployment virtually disappeared, it was accepted firstly that there should be payment to parents for dependent young people over 14 (the school leaving age) and secondly that young people over 16 could receive some National Insurance benefits directly, albeit subject to many limitations (Harris, 1989).

The principle of National Insurance was an important one, because it conferred 'social citizenship' in a particular way. National Insurance meant that individuals contributed towards the cost of their own benefit and this was thought of as a form of social control by providing the worker with a stake in the system. This was very different from the stigmatizing nature of charitable relief or the parish poor relief. However, it applied only to regular workers.

1946–1979: The 'universal' welfare state

The period following the Beveridge Report in 1942 was one in which a universal welfare state was established replacing the old Poor Laws which had existed since Elizabethan times. The welfare state was to provide a right to shelter, health, education, employment and income support for all citizens. Those who found themselves unable to earn an income – the unemployed who had exhausted their insurance contributions or not paid any, the sick, the disabled, the elderly –

received an amount which was based on an assessment of their need rather than on their contribution record. The backbone of this system was still the National Insurance Scheme through which workers contributed to their own income support. The system was, however, still founded on the assumption of a patriarchal model of the nuclear family in which the male wage earner, through full employment, would be able to support his wife and dependants. For young people the age of leaving school, raised to 15 in 1944, was tied for the first time to the eligibility for claiming benefits in their own right (Harris, 1989). As a back-up to National Insurance, National Assistance was introduced – a non-contributory means-tested benefit – which was intended as an interim measure for those who were ineligible for National Insurance. It was assumed that National Insurance would cover most people. Young people were eligible for National Assistance, but since a full employment economy was planned it was thought that they would be unlikely to need to claim it. Although the National Assistance system replaced poor relief, the maintenance of a parallel system of National Insurance meant that people claiming National Assistance were still in danger of being stigmatized, in a two-tier system.

Harris (1989) argues that the Beveridge Report constructed an ambiguous status for young people which was later to provide the opportunity for their independent benefits to be removed. For Beveridge, two classes of young person existed: those who were employed and therefore to some extent independent of parents and those who were in full-time education and therefore deemed to be dependent upon parents. All young people over 15 years of age were expected to be located in one of the two groups: workers or students.

The position of young people not in employment as dependants was recognized by giving benefits to parents rather than to young people. Dependent children under 15, those aged 15 to 18 and still in education, and older non-working children over 15 were provided for by Family Allowance (Family Allowance Act 1945) and Child Tax Allowance, though Family Allowance at this time was not paid for the first child. Provision was extended to cover apprentices after 1956, presumably as a recognition that their 'not-quite-adult' wage status extended their dependency upon their home of origin. Apprenticeship thus became an intermediate status, between dependent child and financially independent worker.

There were further stages of independence, based on economic status and age-grading: according to the Beveridge Report, those who were 15 to 17 years old and unemployed were *partial dependants* upon their parents. The continued system of paying lower wages and lower benefits to this age group assumed that their parents were supporting them. Allowances were age graded: benefits (as well as wages) were different for 16- and 17-year-olds, for 18 to 20-year-olds and for those aged 21 and over. Because those aged under 18 were assumed to be living at home, they were not given an allowance for housing costs, whereas those over 18 were. If young people claimed the dependence allowance themselves, however, they were given one shilling per week less than if their parents claimed on their behalf – this was in order to encourage parents to make the claim. For Beveridge this was 'not a matter of great importance, but it is probably right in view of the fact that boys and girls of this age will be living with older people and while those older people who have earnings can be maintained in part from those earnings' (para 401(F), quoted in Harris, 1989: 55). This legislation, whilst embodying a universal model of citizenship, made assumptions about the dependency status and household relationships of young people, based on their ages and their economic status.

In the 1940s a new distinction was introduced between householders and non-householders. Householders who were living independently were thought to need more money than were non-householders still living at home or in other families. Because of the inclusion of young people in this legislation, the differential between their benefits and those of adults actually widened (Harris, 1989). The householder/non-householder distinction was important because it recognized that some young people did set up independent households.

Under the post-war legislation, young people were recognized as workers, but eligible for National Insurance support only if they had paid sufficient contributions. A 'normative' model of the family and family transitions was assumed in which young people were partial dependants upon the family until they earned sufficient money to leave home and begin a family of their own. The legal age of majority and the conventional 'key to the door' at that time was 21. It was assumed that household and family formation would be covered if necessary by the National Insurance contributions of the male wage earner. The idea of leaving home, getting married or having children without having either a job or an employed male partner with sufficient contributions was inconceivable, and hence no provision was made for this eventuality. National Assistance was only for the unfortunate cases where family support had broken down. Unmarried mothers were a much stigmatized minority, who were expected to enter a special institution, give up their babies for adoption or even in some cases go into a mental asylum. National Assistance was therefore not seen as a means of enabling household and family formation but as a safety net for those not eligible for National Insurance. It was thus based on statuses in youth, rather than processes through youth.

During the 1960s the social security net was widened to include more and more people. The National Insurance Act of 1964 extended Family Allowance to cover dependants up to age 19 in full-time education and National Assistance was replaced in 1966 by Supplementary Benefit, for which the minimum age of entitlement was 16. The previous age bands 16/17, and 18 or over, were however retained, and this still continued the partial dependence of young people under 18 years upon their homes of origin. In 1972 the school-leaving age was raised to 16 – at last corresponding with the age of entitlement to benefits – and a new Child Benefit was introduced to replace the Child Tax Allowance and the Family Allowance. All children including the first child were eligible up to the age of 16, but it was only paid up to the age of 19 if the children were in full-time education. The Family Allowance/Child Benefit was payable to the mother, rather than to the father as income to be pooled, with some recognition that income was not always shared between partners within the household.

With widened criteria for eligibility, and a greater recognition of deprived groups, more and more people were claiming supplementary benefits by the 1970s. Divorce and the rise in the numbers of lone parent families led to a situation where large numbers of people who were not covered by National Insurance were dependent upon Supplementary Benefit. Rising levels of unemployment and longer periods out of work meant that more people, including young people, had exhausted their period of eligibility for National Insurance and had to resort to Supplementary Benefit. The expanding numbers of students were also entitled to Supplementary Benefits during their vacations in the 1970s. Finally, the socio-demographic changes meant that there were more elderly people dependent upon non-contributory benefits. From being a temporary back-up to National Insurance, Supplementary Benefit was now the main source of support for large numbers of claimants.

The normative patterns of household and family formation upon which benefits were based also changed during the 1960s. The age of marriage fell, until one in three brides was a teenager. The cultural autonomy of young people was becoming more visibly asserted through youth cultures. This was also noted in the deliberations of the Latey Committee (1967), which resulted in the lowering of the age of legal majority from 21 to 18 years. Young people were increasingly visible and their independence within society and within their families was gradually gaining public recognition, strengthening their claim to citizenship.

The ideal of universal citizenship through eligibility to welfare did not therefore apply in the way that Marshall had predicted in 1949. His idea of social citizenship, based upon a normative model of 'the nuclear family' with male breadwinner and dependent wife and children was no longer valid (Summers 1991). This ideology of the family had been threatened by demographic and social changes, as we shall show in Chapter 4. Although there were many anomalies – especially in the situation of young people and women, there was a gradual and partial recognition of people as citizens in their own right, rather than with rights derived by proxy through others. This recognition was partly a product of necessity, as many people were not covered by benefits paid to other family members, but it did effect real changes in the rights of young people.

Despite the recognition of individual rights, there were nevertheless attempts to reinforce the normative nuclear family and to ensure its self-sufficiency and privacy. Mothers claiming Supplementary Benefits were encouraged to prosecute the 'liable relative' (the father of their children) for maintenance, but this had a very low rate of success. Women who were believed to have a male partner were expected to be able to be dependent on them, and their Supplementary Benefit was cut accordingly. Young people continued to have an ambiguous status. They, and others not eligible for contributory National Insurance benefits, were subject to the more stigmatizing Social Security in the two-tier system. In all, the increasing demands on the system, and the need for an increased range of benefits to cater for specific needs or specific groups had resulted in a cumbersome and bureaucratic system, in which many people did not know their rights or how to claim them. By the late 1970s the system was under severe strain and in need of reform.

1979–1991: The return to laissez-faire

In 1979, a Conservative Government came into office influenced by the politics of the 'New Right'. It was pledged to cut welfare spending, strengthen the family and root out the so-called 'dependency culture' which, it claimed, had developed with the expansion of the welfare state. By the 1980s, social security was the single largest item of government expenditure, and the proportion of non-contributory benefits had risen as a proportion of the whole social security budget. Social security spending generally had risen from 6 per cent of Gross National Product in 1950 to 13 per cent in 1983 (Halsey, 1988: table 12.27). Young people were an important factor in these figures since they were particularly vulnerable to unemployment and constituted a large proportion of claimants. To the in-coming Conservative Government pledged to cut expenditure, social security – as the single largest item of government expenditure – seemed an obvious target.

One way of saving money was to re-emphasize the patriarchal nuclear family and to force breadwinners to provide for their dependants. The 'radical right' social policy analysts thought that the availability of Supplementary Benefits and state welfare generally – particularly non-contributory benefits – had encouraged irresponsible behaviour sheltered by a 'nanny state' (Abbott and Wallace, 1991). Coupled with this were Malthusian fears of the spread of an 'underclass' of unemployed and lone parent families on welfare reproducing lifestyles of crime and immorality (see Murray, 1990). Influential writers within the 'New Right' recommended that citizenship be defined to mean the obligation of the male worker to support himself and his dependants, thus undermining the rights of those deemed to be dependants (Mead, 1986; Murray, 1986).

By making young people the responsibility of parents rather than the state, expenditure on Supplementary Benefit could be reduced. The philosophy of making young people the responsibility of their families was set out clearly in a leaked cabinet document (*The Guardian*, 17 February 1983) at the beginning of the Thatcher era. It asked:

> What more can be done to encourage families – in the widest possible sense – to reassume responsibilities taken on by the state, for example, responsibility for the disabled, the elderly, unemployed 16-year-olds?

In speeches by the Prime Minister, Margaret Thatcher, parents were exhorted to train their children to save money and prepare for marriage and parenthood. These were seen as traditional family values. Many of these ideas have since been put into practice, as we shall see.

This return to the ideology of the family was a return to what had existed in the welfare system of the 1920s and 1930s. The social security reforms de-legitimized the financial independence which young people had begun to acquire, but at the same time it increased their financial responsibilities. Furthermore, expectations had changed in the intervening period, as had family structures (discussed in Chapter 4). The growth of reconstituted families following divorce (Burgoyne and Clarke, 1984) meant that young people could be forced into dependency on new sets of relatives such as step-parents, and it was not always clear just who was responsible for them. The Children's Act 1990 (see David, 1991) recognizes the rights of children within increasingly complicated family situations where lines of responsibility and authority were unclear. Young people were sometimes cohabiting, having children, and/or getting married before they found jobs. The age at which people enter full-time employment has been getting higher and higher, as Chapter 2 showed. In all, then, the changing structures of families and the changing nature of transitions to adulthood meant that a National Insurance system based upon a male full-time earner with dependent family has become less and less appropriate.

Beveridge's distinction between dependent students and independent workers is no longer sustainable. Increasing numbers of young people are also 'trainees' or 'unemployed'. However, there have been several attempts to make more young people more dependent upon their parents. These include changes in the systems of social security, housing benefits, funding for students, and assistance for those in training and employment.

BENEFIT CHANGES IN THE 1980S

During the 1980s, the Government and its advisers re-defined citizenship as a package of responsibilities rather than automatic rights. People would have to pay for welfare services at the point of delivery, so that all would become aware of the cost of services – parents and patients would have to make more direct payments towards education and health costs, for example, rather than indirectly, through taxation and local rates. Social security was to become more selective and targeted at the most needy. These policies were put into practice, following a review of social security, in the 1986 and 1988 Social Security Acts. Young people were singled out in this legislation for benefit cuts, and their entitlement to some benefits was withdrawn altogether. In the following pages, we shall examine changes in social security legislation and housing assistance, and will also consider recent changes affecting student finance (Table 3.1).

Table 3.1   Benefit changes in the 1980s

Social security
  Income support
  Unemployment benefit
  Severe Hardship payments
  Householder/non-householder distinction abolished

Housing assistance and costs
  Board and lodgings payments
  Non-householder's rent additon
  Non-dependant deduction
  Poll Tax

Student support
  Maintenance grants
  Top-up loans
  Withdrawal of income support
  Withdrawal of housing benefit

Social security legislation

One of the first pieces of legislation carried out by the Conservative Government on coming to power was the introduction of the Social Security Act of 1980. This aimed to cut social security for some groups and 'target' it at those most in need. Young people were not targeted and indeed were one of the groups destined to lose benefit. This was done, first, by introducing a one-to-three month waiting period before supplementary benefits could be claimed by school leavers. This was to discourage people from signing on during their holidays before starting a job or returning to school after claiming for the holiday period. However, parents could claim extended child benefit during this period. Secondly, students in non-advanced further education were excluded from claiming benefits. Thirdly, Exceptional Needs payments, which had been available to young people to help them set up a new home, were severely curtailed. Young people had to show that they had unsuccessfully sought furnished rented accommodation before they could claim payments for essential furniture. This was one of the ways in which it was intended to prevent young people from setting up home 'on the dole' and to keep them within their families.

There was a gradual erosion of young people's entitlement to benefits throughout the 1980s but the major reforms took place as a result of the Social Security legislation which came into force in 1988 following the Fowler Review of Social Security in 1985. Under this legislation, which was intended to be the main reform of the principles of social security since Beveridge, entitlement to Supplementary Benefit (renamed Income Support) was withdrawn from 16- and 17-year-olds on the assumption that they would be provided places on training schemes (Roll, 1990). This was estimated to have deprived 90 000 young people from claiming benefit (Stewart and Stewart, 1988). Parents were still able to claim Child Benefit until their children were nineteen years of age if they were in full-time education and could claim 'Family Credit', paid to the head of the household (usually the father), for children if they were in work but on low incomes. In other words, it was once again up to parents to claim on their children's behalf. Since the take-up of the means-tested Family Credit is low, in practice its introduction has meant a loss of income for poorer families, in comparison with when young people claimed their own benefits.

From 1988 onwards, benefits were linked more clearly to training allowances. There was a £15 per week 'bridging allowance' (for a maximum of eight weeks) whilst a young person waited for a training place. Under exceptional circumstances, such as if they had a child or were disabled and were therefore ineligible for work, or if they could prove that they could not live with their parents, 16- and 17-year-olds could claim Income Support. In the face of increasing criticism of these regulations and the hardships they imposed, the Government introduced 'Severe Hardship' payments for 16- and 17-year-olds. Though many young people are not aware of these payments and like many means-tested benefits they are difficult to claim, there were 27 000 applications in 1990 (MORI, 1991). Entitlement is at the discretion of the Minister and there is great variation between local offices in response to claims. As Kirk and colleagues (1991) have pointed out even these benefits have been allowed to erode with inflation.

The householder/non-householder distinction introduced in the 1940s was abolished in 1988 and was replaced by one based on age: 25 was chosen as the age at which the adult rate of benefit could be paid on the assumption that young people were more likely to be living at home until then. Far from reflecting the real pattern of leaving home (described in Chapter 5), this was an arbitrary distinction. Couples under the age of 25 received less than those over that age, but the difference for young people with children above and below age 25 was removed after protest from the Church of England, the Social Security Advisory Committee and other lobbies (Harris, 1989; Roll, 1990).

The changes were designed to ensure that young people would return to their families for support and that young women should not get pregnant as a strategy for getting housed – although there is no evidence to support the latter argument (see Chapter 5). However, it assumed that parents were indeed there to support them. This represented a further shift away from benefits paid directly to young people and towards benefits paid to parents on their behalf.

Housing assistance

The right of young people to set up independent households had previously been recognized with an allowance for additional costs in the rate of Supplementary Benefits from the Department of Social Security (DSS), by the payment of rent and the cost of board and lodgings by the DSS for those out of work, and by the means-tested payment of Housing Benefit by local authorities towards rent.

In parallel with the changes in the 1980s described above, there were changes in support for those living away from home, which were also intended to encourage young people who were in financial difficulty to return to their family home. Their scope for leaving home had already been limited by the shortage of suitable accommodation and the structure of the housing market (see Chapter 6). Now their means of access to accommodation was also restricted through a re-definition of entitlement to benefits. The higher 'householder' rate of benefit, which young people living independently had previously claimed, was abolished for young people aged under 26 in 1987. (Youth Training allowances do not include a housing cost element either, as we pointed out in Chapter 2, and hence it is also more difficult for those on schemes to leave home.) From 1983, 16- and 17-year-olds lost the contribution towards their 'board' included in the non-householder benefit (the non-householder's rent addition), and this was withdrawn from the 18 to 20 age group in 1984, and from the 21 to 24 age group in 1986. The benefits they received no longer recognized the cost of living at home, though the rent addition had never reflected the actual patterns of board payments by children to their parents (Jones, 1991a). The cost of keep was expected to be fully met by their parents if they were living at home; this particularly affected poorer families who may have depended upon a contribution from children to the household budget.

Parents on low incomes or unemployed and claiming Housing Benefit, with employed children living at home, had their benefit reduced on the assumption that their working children would be making a contribution towards the household rent (this was known as the 'non-dependant deduction'). So under these circumstances, young workers were supposed to be contributing to the housing costs of their families even though there was no acknowledgement of this in training or income support allowances. Again, age-grading formed the basis of the policy, and the deductions from parents' benefit varied with the age of their working children.

In the same way as the family means test of the 1930s assumed that income within the household was redistributed from one family member to another, this legislation, too, assumed a redistribution of income within the household. It assumed that money is negotiated and shared within the household according to some kind of 'rational model' (Carling, 1991). It assumed that if parents were given money towards the cost of keeping children, that is what they would spend it on. It assumed that working children with unemployed parents would contribute towards their parents' housing cost. This model of the household and the rational negotiation of household income, is of course an abstract assumption. It has never been investigated or proven. Nor is it consistent: two different models of dependency exist within Housing Benefit and Income Support regulations (Jones, 1991a).

The changes in the Board and Lodgings regulations were another attempt to force young people who had left home, to return to their families rather than claim benefit if they ran into trouble. Again, age has been introduced as a criterion for access to benefits and people below the age of 26 are singled out for harsher treatment. The changes in the Board and Lodgings regulations began from rumours initiated by the *Sun* newspaper that unemployed youngsters were living it up in 'Costa del Dole' seaside towns during the summer months. In fact, there was no evidence for this claim. Other concerns emerged, however. First, there was the danger of exploitation by landlords who were able to charge an exorbitant price for lodgings, knowing that the DSS would pick up the bill. Then there was also concern that since most young people's wage levels could not possibly cover such rents, this could act as a work disincentive. In 1980 a maximum rent was defined, over which the DSS would not pay, and in 1983 a three-tier system of payment was introduced for different kinds of accommodation and claimant circumstances. Claims for payment under the Board and Lodgings regulations nevertheless rose dramatically, with an increase of 60 per cent in claims by those aged under 25, compared with an increase of 25 per cent overall (Harris, 1989). The reaction of the Government was to reduce the amount of Income Support payable at the non-householder's rate after between two and four weeks. Young people were allowed a period of grace in which to find somewhere else to live. This was applied to all claimants under 26 years.

Various appeals against this regulation in 1986 were upheld in court; the regulations were deemed unlawful and the Government had to repay benefits owed to at least 17 000 claimants. However, it had already instituted changes in the law so that despite the success of the appeals, the Board and Lodgings regulations relating to young people were introduced in 1986, compelling young people to move on after four to six weeks (Harris, 1989).

From 1989, rents were met entirely by Local Authority Housing Benefit rather than the DSS. This discouraged landlords from renting to young people because their rents were paid in arrears whereas landlords wanted them in advance. Under the Social Security Act 1988, the amount of Housing Benefit payable was also reduced. A new maximum of up to 35 per cent of rent and up to 80 per cent of rates (later Community Charge or 'Poll Tax') was gradually introduced. The introduction of the Poll Tax, so called unofficially because it was a levy on individuals over the age of 18, meant that for the first time young people living at home had to pay towards the costs of local services, and this applied even if they were not in employment. Under the old system, rates had been charged to household heads, and thus only young people who had left home were expected to pay.

The Poll Tax, now to be re-vamped, was once the flagship of the Conservative administration and embodied a new definition of citizenship (Miller, 1989). Introduced under the Local Government Finance Act 1988, it defined citizenship in terms of responsibilities as well as rights, including the responsibility to pay for services. Civil duties were linked with political rights. Since the age of paying was also the age of adult suffrage, local authorities would be more answerable to their local citizens. We should note, however, that the age of conferring *civil* and *political* citizenship, in this sense, was different to that of conferring rights of *social* citizenship, such as Income Support.

The subsequent modification of the Poll Tax reflects not the fact that this model has been abandoned, but rather that a less strident and more pragmatic attempt to collect local taxes and maintain popularity has been adopted using the same principles.

Student support

Students have been able to receive income from a variety of sources: from parents, from their own work, from local authority maintenance grants (which are means-tested and make up the main source of student finance) and from Housing Benefit (until 1990) as well as from social security (in some cases).

During the post-war period more and more young people have been staying at school beyond the minimum school-leaving age and more are continuing into higher education. There is, as we discussed in Chapter 2, a problem over who is going to pay for them. The 'Robbins principle', of a right to higher education supported by a grant system, was eroded. Though the right to higher education was preserved, there was no longer an automatic right to state support, and access to social citizenship in this context has become more restricted. Instead, there was a shifting line between support by parents, self-support and support by the state. Student fees are paid by the local authority of the student's home of origin. Since 1964, students accepted for a higher education place have received a mandatory maintenance grant, which is sufficient to support them away from home if necessary. Those over the age of 25 can receive a higher rate of grant to reflect their 'mature' status, but also if they are below this age and have been in employment for a substantial amount of time, or if they have lived extensively away from home and can be deemed 'independent'. Those who are married or cohabiting, are means-tested on their partner's income.

Most of the rest are at least partly dependent on parental contributions. The grant is paid after a means-test on the parental income, and a wider and wider group of parents has been required to contribute since the 1970s in a process of 'fiscal drag', as the value of the grant has been allowed to decline with inflation. In the early days of the maintenance grant, students could supplement their incomes by claiming supplementary benefits during the vacations. However, the amounts were limited, and in 1986–7 the entitlement was removed during the short vacations and from 1991 also for the long vacations. The maintenance grant was increased by £36 to compensate for this loss of benefit and costs of travel and books were disregarded as part of the grant in assessing claims during the long vacation. It is assumed that students should support themselves through jobs in the long vacations or be supported by parents. The message was clear – students should be getting more support from parents rather than the state. However, one in three parents did not pay their contribution towards maintenance grants, and the 20 per cent decline in the real value of student grants since they began meant that students often lived on private overdrafts from banks for much of their higher education careers – according to one study 64 per cent were in debt by the end of the Christmas term (Harris, 1989). To obviate this, 'top-up loans' were introduced in 1990 to a maximum of £420 per person. Other support was withdrawn too: students were no longer allowed to claim Housing Benefit (previously paid by the local authority in the area of their college) at the same rate from 1988 – only 35 per cent of rent could be claimed if they were under 25 years (and they also had to pay at least 20 per cent of the new Community Charge). Thus the overall support for students has been reduced and the costs shifted first from the state to the parents, and then from the parents to the individual student. The argument is that if they are to benefit from higher education in the long term as individuals, then they should have to pay for it as individuals. This reflects the Government's over-all view that welfare should be paid by the consumer (Barr, 1989).

An alternative model of paying for higher education was that intro-duced in Australia, where a 'graduate tax' introduced in 1988 sought to shift the burden of payment very squarely onto the individual not through loans and overdrafts but by deductions from their subse-quent earnings as a 'graduate tax'. This is the system recommended by Barr (1989) as a fairer one. The whole-scale transfer of respon-sibility to individuals practised in Australia is more publicly account-able and does not depend for its success upon private family negotiations and transactions.

Some students below the age of 18 are entitled to Educational Main-tenance Grants, although this varies widely between different local authorities and Harris (1989) estimates that only one in ten students outside higher education receive such grants. Under the '21-hour rule' some students were able to study part-time whilst claiming supple-mentary benefits and this was encouraged by a campaign by Youthaid, a pressure group for young people. The 21-hour rule for non-advanced further education was also tightened up, although some colleges responded by designing courses around students' bene-fit entitlement. The consequence of these changes is that students in all sectors of education increasingly support themselves through part-time working (see Chapter 2).

Young people of all social backgrounds – students who are middle class, as well as working-class school leavers – are thus hit by changes in the re-definition of responsibility for young people. The responsibility for paying for students has not only been privatized by transferring responsibility to families and sponsorship and away from the state, but has been individualized as well: young people are required to pay for their own higher and further education. It is seen as an individual responsibility leading to an individual benefit. The wealth and generosity of parents remain, however, important factors; while state provision can have an equalizing effect in this respect, the new system is likely to lead to elitism on the one hand, where parents can use their wealth, and to poverty and debt on the other hand, where families have no wealth to pass on. It remains to be seen what effect the changes in student support will have on entry to higher education.

CITIZENSHIP BY PROXY?

National Insurance and other income support strategies in the immediate post-war period were based upon the assumption that people (especially men) held regular, full-time employment careers and that women and young people lived in conventional nuclear families supported by a household head. They assumed that employment and the family serviced one another in a set of regulated transitions. Thus, the employed male head of household supported his dependants, and resources were shared within the household. Social citizenship rights of women and children were thus derived indirectly from the head of household. As we see throughout this book, these assumptions are hard to sustain in the present age, when – as following chapters will indicate – families do not conform to the normative nuclear structure, when transactions and negotiations within families are known to be complex and problematic, and when young people's transitions into employment and independent housing have been re-structured by the changing conditions outside the home. Lister (1990, 1991) has cogently argued the case for women's contribution within the household as well as in the labour market, to be more fully acknowledged, so that women can fully participate in society as citizens. In the current debate on citizenship, no such demands have been made by, or on behalf of, young people. It is not only young people's contributions and responsibilities within the home which have been overlooked, but also their relationship to the labour market while they are trainees – a status which carries little financial recognition while they are in training, and no entitlement to National Insurance when they leave. Paradoxically, the right to training and education has been extended whilst the support for those who are taking these routes has declined.

In the contemporary context, young people have been constructed as a special category of persons with reduced rights to social security and little power to demand more. This situation has become possible, because as we have seen in tracing the history of benefits, young people's separate eligibility has never really been fully recognized. Furthermore, since they are not fully eligible for contributory National Insurance in their own right they have had to depend upon National Assistance, Supplementary Benefits and Income Support. Their access to social citizenship rights under these non-contributory benefits can be more easily challenged. The recent changes in social security have been designed to force young people back into their families on the assumption that their families can and will support them. However, whilst some families do support them, others do not. The consequence has been increased poverty for many young people and for their families, increasing dependence upon families and the emerging problem of indebtedness (as we shall see in the following chapters).

Seen over a longer-term perspective, young people's position with social security systems, whilst fragile, was becoming 'individualized': they were increasingly acknowledged as individuals. The changes introduced in the 1980s therefore represent a regressive step away from individualization by extending dependence in youth. They also parallel other state interventions in education, training and the labour market. This places particular hardships on poorer families. Furthermore, it is doubtful that any welfare system can cope with criteria for eligibility which fully takes account of individual needs. We suggested at the start of this chapter that it may be difficult in practice to legislate for the 'welfare transition' in youth from receiving benefits by proxy to receiving direct benefits in one's own right. The Severe Hardship payments are an example of this. It has been necessary to accept that there are circumstances where age is not a criterion of dependence, and where a system of entitlement based on prescribed age-grading cannot work: young people aged 16 and 17 may not, for a variety of reasons, be able to be dependent on their parents or able to derive social citizenship rights through them. The age of entitlement to social citizenship in this context is 18, but it has to be acknowledged that there are circumstances where direct access to social citizenship is needed before then. The 'missing ingredient' in the social security criteria of need is any recognition of varying domestic circumstances: in other words, young people's rights and responsibilities in the domestic sphere.

Within the social security system, there have been two sets of criteria which have structured eligibility. The first is economic status and we saw how the welfare system has now reduced its coverage to exclude young workers, students, and even most of the otherwise unemployed with the introduction of trainee status (it is thus left with practically no responsibility for the 16 to 18 age group, apart from young mothers). The second set of criteria is associated with age, and we have seen how benefits are increasingly based on age-grading. This means that social security is based on assumptions about age-related status and responsibilities, rather than on need criteria. Policies should indeed take account of process when assessing young people's entitlements, but age is not necessarily the most appropriate indicator of this. In order to understand the processes underlying young people's transitions to economic independence and their financial needs we have to enter the 'private world' of family life.

4

DEPENDENCE ON

THEIR FAMILIES?

Formal institutions, on the one hand, are creating structures through which young people pass as they become adult, and within which recognition must eventually occur if they are to become full citizens. On the other hand, informal relationships within families provide an immediate context within which transitions to adulthood are shaped. In this book, we consider the various, and often conflicting, pressures that seek to shape the lives of young people as they become adult, pressures which stem from the private world of family life and from the public world of state policies and market forces. So far, our focus has been on the 'public sphere', changing structures which determine official categories of dependence and independence, and issues of choice and constraint, conformity and resistance. In this chapter, we focus more on individual and (to some extent) family biographies rather than the history of formal structures and consider the ways in which public policies and institutions may affect the 'private sphere'. We shall examine how, though this is usually unacknowledged in public policy, dependent children begin the process of transition to economic independence while still living in their family homes. Our focus is on the social and economic relationships between young people and their parents, and the ways in which these relationships change, over time and during the early life course.

First we examine the ways in which family and household structures have changed in history and consider the types of families in which young people currently grow up, in terms of their composition and external and internal economic relationships. Then, we consider the social and economic elements of the parent–child relationship, including the role of parents as providers and that of children as recipients. We look at how these 'roles' change, and offer a critique of the simplistic notions of dependence and independence which as we have seen underlie both functionalist perspectives on family life and social policies affecting young people and families. We consider the power structures within families which affect their functioning and the functioning of their members. Finally, we highlight aspects of the parent–child relationship which current social policies seek to change.

In 1987, Margaret Thatcher proffered the view that 'there is no such thing as society; there are only individual men and women and there are families'. Between families, the inequalities of social class, economic status, race and region are continually structuring differences in the way that families function and family members' expectations of one another. The focus here on intra-family relationships cannot lose sight of structural inequalities therefore. Even within families, the structural inequalities of gender, age and generation still of course apply. Marital endogamy frequently occurs: people tend to marry partners of the same social class or educational level as themselves (Jones, 1990b) and there are rarely clear social class inequalities within families as a result (viz. McRae, 1986). But there are inequalities between marriage partners resulting from gender relations and the gender division of labour in the household. Within the parent–child relationship, there are inequalities associated with age and generation, aspects of which are gradually redressed as the young person grows up (Harris, 1983: 247):

> What is required, if the place of the family in industrial societies is to be better understood, is that a new generation of studies come into existence which examines the pattern of relations between the private and public domains and regards the household as the site of their articulation.

Studies which have since examined the relationship between the public and the private domains over the last decade have focused on marital relationships. We want to extend this analysis to the relationship between parents and their adolescent or adult children.

We should emphasize first an important point. The parent–child relationship may not be the most important or significant relationship in a child's life. Other family members inside or outside the household, including siblings or grandparents (Cunningham-Burley, 1985; Finch, 1989), may have an important role in mediating (or substituting for) parent–child relations, as might other people outside the kinship network, such as friends, neighbours or those whose relationship with a young person is a professional one, as in the case of teachers, social workers, employers and so on. The significance of many of these relationships may change as a young person grows up:

friendships may be replaced by (or become) partnerships, and families of origin may be left as young people form new families of their own. In other words, youth is a period during which many relationships are changing and many new ones are developing. Our focus on parent–child relations must not lose sight of the wider social context in which they occur.

DEMOGRAPHIC AND HISTORICAL CHANGE

First, we need to consider the changes in family structure, the changes in the relationship (particularly the economic relationship) between families and the wider society, and the changes in intra-family relationships which have occurred over time. These three aspects are inter-connected.

Pre-industrial and industrial society

Family structures and relationships alter with changes in the material and cultural basis of the wider society (Allan, 1985). Thus, there appear to have been many changes in family structure in the period of urbanization following the Industrial Revolution. It has been argued that the twin processes of urbanization, involving geographical mobility, and industrialization (with its attendant centralization of production and formalization of paid labour), together removed the collective production role from families, so that the family unit's articulation with society was mediated increasingly through consumption (Weber, 1961), through social reproduction, or through the productive role of the male head of household and 'breadwinner' (Parsons and Bales, 1956; Goode, 1970). According to Weber, the Industrial Revolution, in cutting the link between the family unit and production, created a schism between the public and private worlds. There are resulting images, prevalent in the functionalist literature of the 1950s and 1960s, of the pre-industrial family as a large household which included members of the extended family, in contrast to the 'modern' nuclear family comprising typically a dominant bread-winning husband, a subordinate wife and their dependent children (Parsons and Bales, 1956; Goode, 1970).

Demographic and historical research have shown in recent years that both the image of family life in pre-industrial society and that of family life in industrial society are based on myth rather than reality. Families in pre-industrial times were no larger than now: confusion had arisen because of the use of the terms 'family' and 'household' interchangeably, since many pre-industrial households, particularly those of the rich, contained servants who lived as household members, but were not necessarily kin (Flandrin, 1979; see also Chapter 5). Most households immediately prior to the Industrial Revolution averaged five persons and consisted of parents and their children. The 'nuclear family' was not therefore a result of industrialization, according to Laslett (1972).

Nor can it be said that the extended family is becoming less significant in the present day. Bell (1968) has shown the importance of the extended middle-class family, simultaneously dismissing the myths that the supportive extended family was a working-class pattern, and the view that industrialization and the extended family could not co-exist. Weber argued that the separation of the social from the economic, of landownership from the household, was central to the development of a rational capitalist system. MacFarlane (1978) challenged the whole argument that families had become separated from the economic system, and Ray Pahl (1984) has revealed the extent to which families were acting as co-operatives within the informal labour market in ways which appeared to be a continuation of pre-industrial patterns (see also Owen, 1987, for a discussion of the parallel roles of husbands and wives). It was the false separation of the world into public and private domains which had hidden the productive function of modern families from view. A polarization was identified by Pahl, however, between families with members in employment which were involved in various forms of work, and those where no one was employed or working in the informal market. The ability to operate as a collective was therefore stratified, but 'once households get into a benign spiral upwards their collective efforts keep them there' (Pahl, 1984: 334).

Marriage at least can thus be seen as an economic partnership, reflecting (Leonard, 1980:4):

> a move away from seeing the family as a 'unit of consumption' and psychic support, with relationships between 'individuals', to a stress on production and reproduction within the family and the wider society ...

We can take this process further by looking at the parent–child relationship in this light, focusing on the material and economic aspects of their relationship. Many of the arguments relating to the dependency of female partners on their male spouses, can also be applied to the status of young people in their families of origin. For example, just as gender inequalities enacted in the home nevertheless derive from the differing relations of marriage partners to the production process (Harris, 1983), so age inequalities in the home can be seen to relate to economic roles in the 'external world'.

There were many real changes in family life in recent decades. Though there was no schism between the public and private worlds, as Weber had suggested, there was nevertheless increased privatism of family life, particularly among the working class (Goldthorpe *et al.*, 1969, Pahl and Wallace, 1988). It was suggested that people were wanting more privacy in their home lives, but as Allan and Crow (1988) have argued, the changes that took place were more complex. The changes in education and the labour market discussed in Chapter 2, and the changes in the benefit system discussed in Chapter 3, have all had their impact on family life, sometimes causing financial hardship and increased strain on families. Furthermore, new forms of housing design in the 1960s, such as high-rise blocks, and new forms of consumption involving indoor activities, such as watching television, have also changed family life. There was increased strain on family relationships (Komarovsky, 1967: 340; Cohen, 1972: 17). Families became more vulnerable. The 'primary' relationships within families (husband–wife and/or parent–child; see Harris, 1983) were the most likely to come under strain, and we see some consequences of this in the higher rate of divorce and the greater number of children who have experienced the breakdown of their parents' relationship (Fogelman, 1976) and sometimes, in consequence, the breakdown of their own relationship with one of their parents.

'Post-industrial' society

It has been suggested that we are now in a post-industrial age, in which many of the structures of industrial society are reforming or even disappearing, and that family structures have changed further as a result. So what kinds of families do young people live in nowadays? The normative nuclear family appears to be under threat: there are fewer of them. An analysis of the 1981 Census, found that only about one in ten of households conformed to a strict definition of nuclear family type (Bernardes, 1986).

The most significant change in recent decades has probably been in the increased labour force participation of women, so that the likelihood now is that married women with dependent children will be in employment and therefore have additional roles to those of homemaker, domestic labourer and carer. This means that it is more obviously inappropriate to think of the family as articulated to the wider society through the male head of household as 'sole breadwinner'; there is an increased likelihood that for a variety of reasons he may not exist.

Family studies have emphasized the increased diversity of family life (Kiernan and Wicks, 1990), with increasing numbers of births outside marriage, more frequent cohabitation between non-married partners, more one-person households, divorce and re-constituted families (consisting of step-siblings as well as step-parents). One consequence is that extended families and kinship networks have become larger (Wicks, 1991). It could be argued that individuals have more choice about which of their kin relations they acknowledge and develop; that kin relationships are therefore less prescriptive. These new forms appear to contrast with earlier patterns. Interpretations of change have varied, however: some commentators emphasize the disintegration of traditional patterns, while others, like Giddens (1991), argue that families are being re-constructed. There are other cases where old family forms are clearly being re-defined, rather than changed, as societal approbation of 'alternative' living arrangements has decreased. Campaigners for the rights of children, women, gays and lesbians, for example, have had some effect in shifting public opinion to reduce the stigma attached to illegitimacy, cohabitation, bachelorhood and homosexuality.

These changes mean that although most young people have had experience of normative family structure (two generations, consisting of parents and children) *at some stage in their lives*, there are increasing numbers who experience family dissolution and consequently non-nuclear family structures. Kiernan and Wicks (1990) suggest that if trends continue, 20 per cent of present-day children will experience a parental divorce by the age of 16, and they report that 14 per cent of all families with dependent children are headed by lone parents, mainly lone mothers. It is becoming more common to have step-parents and step-siblings, and step-extended families, or, because of the difficulties associated with some of these experiences and new relationships, to have moved to live with grandparents or other relatives, or in some cases to be received into local authority care.

Wilson and Pahl (1988) argue that although relatively few households are of the strictly conventional nuclear family structure, the family does exist, but 'is best understood as a system of relationships that change over time'. As Finch (1989) points out, moreover, though household structures have changed, the moral ties of family relationships remain strong in the present day. As we indicate, the vast majority of people have some experience of a parent–child relationship, for example, even if this is not with their natural parents. It has become increasingly clear, though, that as social scientists we should be cautious about referring to 'The Family' as though an individual's current experience of family life conformed to this normative idea.

State intervention

Many of the changes in family life over the last century have occurred, either directly or indirectly, as a result of state interventions, often pre-dating the introduction of the welfare state. Morgan (1985) has discussed the ways in which legislation and official ideologies have structured family relationships through legal definitions of 'irreconcilable marital breakdown', the 'broken home' and 'the family unit', and through approaches to the concept of the family wage, taxation and social security policies. We noted in Chapter 3 that the welfare state was structured around a functionalist view of 'The Family'.

Over the last hundred years there has been state intervention in the parent–child relationship, and the development of an ideology of 'good parenting', for example with the introduction of health visitors to monitor the care of very young children, and with the development of welfare agencies whose function is to protect children from parental abuse. Expertise in child care has been developed outside the family, and parental skills once considered to be instinctual and natural have been professionalized (Mayall, 1990). The result is an often uneasy relationship between parents and representatives of state institutions, such as teachers, social workers and health workers, in which parents feel de-skilled and dis-empowered.

According to the child-care legislation, parents are responsible for the physical, emotional, intellectual, social and moral development of their children. The role demands that parents provide both support and control; failure is likely to be monitored. Harris (1983: 241) comments on the dominant child–rearing ideology and the resulting position of parents:

> If the parent is seen to be socially responsible for the character of the child; if the child's behaviour is regarded as a measure of the moral and personal worth of the parent, then the power of the child becomes enormous. By its behaviour it can determine the respect according to its parents by their significant others and the self-image of the parents themselves. But if the child has so much power, then it can use that power effectively to diminish the area of parental control. Quite apart from the influence of others on the child, and quite apart from the content of the dominant child-rearing ideology, the domain assumption of modern child-rearing: parents are responsible for the characters of their children, itself effectively deprives them of the degree of control over their children which they need if they are to discharge that responsibility.

Parental ability to control is closely associated with the dependency status of their children – an issue which we will discuss here – and the dependence of young people on their families has also been structured by state interventions, ranging from limitations on and regulations concerning child labour, to the Education Acts which extended state educational provision (see Chapter 2) to the regulations and ideologies underlying structures of social security and national assistance (see Chapter 3). Over the last century, the institutionalization of childhood and extension of education in particular have extended the period of economic dependency of young people.

Finch (1989: 72) points out that the growth of state intervention in the nineteenth century to control the employment of children and establish and expand compulsory education, had the effect of altering the balance of obligations between parents and their children, and thus the economic functioning of families. As it became more difficult for children to make a contribution from their earnings to the family budget, childhood and youth became established as a period of one-way economic dependence (see Anderson, 1980). Even then, the situation was not clear-cut – children who earned money while still at school were still expected to hand their earnings over as part of the household income (Jamieson, 1986, quoted in Finch, 1989), and there were still opportunities for young people to contribute in non-financial terms to the household economy, such as through providing child care and doing housework. Economic dependency was therefore not necessarily total.

'Traditional family values'

'The Family' is currently under the political spotlight. The role of 'the traditional family' as the 'building block of society' is blindly upheld, and seen as the epitome of all that is good. The stress on 'traditional values' is based on the model of the patriarchal nuclear family and traditional gender roles (see, for example, Scruton, 1986), rather than empirical evidence about the nature of family life either in history or in the present day.

The ideology of the patriarchal nuclear family has been at the forefront of Government policy during the 1980s. According to the 'New Right' version of this ideology, the power of the state over young people has been increasing and the power of the family has weakened; the result has been an increase in juvenile crime and deviancy. The answer, according to Marsland (1986) is to withdraw state benefits, and make young people economically dependent on their parents, thus reinforcing the traditional values of family life. In consequence, policies have increased the pressure on parents to support their young financially (Marsland, 1986: 94):

> Young people need the support of their families and the family is
> seriously weakened as an institution if it loses its responsibility
> for young people. But genuine family responsibility for young

people is make believe unless at least some of the costs of their care are shifted back from the state to the family.

Nowhere in this thinking is there any consideration of how the process of emancipation from parental control and the transition to economic independence are supposed to occur, or how, in order for young people to grow up, parental responsibility for them can be allowed to diminish. Nor, of course, does it consider the problem created for many families when the period of youth is continually extended. While claiming to remove state control from the lives of young people, the 'New Right' are in practice increasing the state control of family relationships (and of course continuing to maintain power over the lives of the young if only indirectly via their parents). The increased pressure on parents could become untenable: are they to continue to accept additional responsibilities for longer periods, as though the household budget were a bottomless pit? Recent policies affecting social security regulations would appear to take this view, as we have shown.

What we often see is a conflict between young people's attempts to become economically independent and emancipated from the control of their parents, and the policies of the state which can actively discourage any such moves.

PARENT–CHILD RELATIONSHIPS

We shall now examine some of the elements in the relationship between parents and their adolescent children, concentrating on issues of control and economic dependency (and their counterparts, emancipation and economic independence) within the domestic context. We examine the changing relationships between parents and their children, and the extent to which parents enable young people to become independent adults, through studying the roles of parental advice, pocket money and gifts. We consider the part young people play in the household economy, in the form of payment towards the cost of their board and keep and the work they are involved in around the home (Table 4.1). We consider the processes involved in the transition from dependent child to independent adult in terms of the economic and power relations these terms represent. The tensions and ambivalences associated with many of the negotiations which are involved are discussed. Finally, the role of the state will be reexamined and we will suggest that although young people make great moves towards adult status while living with their families, their progress is not always acknowledged by the public institutions of the state. Despite the public rhetoric about the need for independence, in

Table 4.1 Parent–child economic exchanges

Parent to child	*Child to parent*
Pocket money	Board money
Payment for work	Payment towards rent
Gifts	Help in family firm
Advice on	Work in the home
leaving school and jobs	housework and child care
leaving home and housing	gardening and decorating

practice, state policy is based on a static vision of family roles which takes no account of process and does not encourage emancipation and independence in youth.

While we recognize the variety of situations in which young people grow up, we are concentrating here on parent–child relationships in families living together under one roof. This is the situation that most people experience for at least part of their childhood. It is important also to recognize that the relationships between parents and children will vary according to the sex of each (Mayall, 1990). Where possible, we try to maintain these distinctions here, defining parent–child relations as the varied and changing age, generation and gender relations between parents and their children. 'The parent' is thus not one kind of person in one kind of role; parents, like their children, vary by age, sex, class, ethnicity, employment status and according to many other variables in the parts they play in the social world. Such concerns do not apparently trouble policy-makers, the media, and others who speak of 'parental responsibility', when seeking to draw the boundary of responsibility between 'the family' and the state.

Growing up in their families

Many aspects of the relationship between parents and their children have an economic basis, and the issue of dependence in childhood is problematic. It is legitimated, however, by the public/private dichotomy, as women's dependency has been, according to Lister (1990). The 'black box' of the family has now been opened to a great extent where the position of wives is now concerned, particularly in the research that has been done on the financial arrangements of marriage partners (for example, by Pahl, 1989), and this is reflected in recent changes in taxation policies which now treat married women in the same way as married men. When it comes to the young, however, it seems that the black box remains firmly closed, at least in terms of the prevailing government ideology of 'the family'. According to this ideology, young people living in their parental homes are economically dependent on their parents. The ideology obscures current practice but nevertheless underpins current Government policies.

It is important to examine the family and home context of young people's lives. It is the base from which they grow up. It provides a model for their own separate adult lives, though not necessarily one which they will follow. It provides both a launching pad and people to leave (a locus for ritual and symbolism). Processes of transition, social and economic, begin within the family of origin, and recognition of elements of adult status is likely to come first from family members. Becoming adult solely in the eyes of family members is, however, problematic, since adult status also needs to be publicly confirmed by a variety of institutions in a variety of settings outside the family context. Until a young adult enters and is accepted by the institutions of the labour market, the state benefit system, the housing market and the consumer market place, their adulthood cannot be socially confirmed.

We need then to examine some of the ways in which the relationship between young people and their parents changes with age, involving shifts in the power relationship, and also shifts in the economic relationship between parents and their children. These twin aspects of familial relations we see as crucial to understanding the family context of the transitions to adult independence. They involve negotiation, cause tension and are surrounded with ambiguity.

Parental advice

One of the main functions of parents as children become adolescent is to help them to become independent (Parsons, 1956) – a role about which parents tend to be very ambivalent. Nevertheless, parents often advise their children on moves linked with the transition to adulthood – moves which may have implications for the domestic economy. For example, children may turn to their parents for advice about whether to stay on at school, or whether to leave and get a job; whether to continue to live at home, or whether to leave the area for better jobs or educational opportunities elsewhere. Jamieson's (1987) historical study of people who had grown up between the two world wars found that there were cases where young people left school not from choice, but because their families needed their wages. This may still be the case, according to Wallace (1987a) and Griffin (1985).

The parents' ability to provide appropriate help will largely depend on their own experience. It is not surprising therefore that children who stay on in education beyond the minimum school leaving age usually have parents who did so (Halsey *et al.*, 1980) or that there is an association between parents' occupations and the industry in which they work and that of their children (though this is particularly between fathers and sons, mainly because of the changing nature of women's participation in the labour market). One outcome is intergenerational stability of occupational class positions (Jones, 1987a), but as a result of similar mechanisms, unemployment can also run in families (Payne, 1987).

The system of recruiting new workers through contacts with current employees has been well documented as a means by which an employer can ensure compliance in the work force (see Jenkins *et al.*, 1983). Allatt and Yeandle (1986) also suggest, however, that the practice has implications for power relationships within families, since it increases a young person's sense of obligation to a parent. Despite the fact that the Careers Service, Youth Training schemes, schools career teachers, and so on, have been specifically provided as sources of job advice and information for young people, school leavers still depend to a great extent on receiving informal information about jobs: one-third of men and over a quarter of women in the National Child Development Study (NCDS) reported that their source of information about their first jobs was a relative or friend (Jones, 1986). Widespread unemployment tends to lead at first to an even greater dependence on kin for job information, but as the labour market contracts, and parents themselves lose their jobs, the system breaks down (Morris, 1987). Allatt and Yeandle (1986) show how one's own immediate family obligations to help with job information may structure the willingness to help extended kin, in a time of economic recession and job shortages, while at the same time, dormant kinship relationships may be revived and tested. In practice, unemployment is thus often clustered in families, partly also because unemployment is clustered in local labour markets.

There are thus some circumstances in which parents cannot provide appropriate help for their children. Some parents are not in a position to advise their adult children, because they are not in possession of adequate information, where, for example, they are unemployed, or employed in a declining industry, or where opportunities are not locally based, or where options are new-founded and do not relate to parents' own experience (such as with many of the new educational or training provisions). In the latter case, parents are particularly 'de-skilled' when changes in the labour market or in the social security system are not only new to their experience, but also happening at too fast a pace to assimilate. In these cases particularly, young people may have to depend on help from the more formal sources of information provided by the state, and family relationships may be weakened as a result.

Pocket money and gifts

During the period of dependent childhood, most parents make material provision for their children – they provide a home, food, clothing –
as well as emotional support, a frame of reference, and an identity.
Provision gradually decreases as young people begin to start part-time
work and buy some of their own clothes, learn to cook, do some
housework or other jobs around the home, and generally learn some
of the skills of self-care and adult independent living, while still under
the overall care and protection of their parents.

Parents generally provide some financial help to their children in
the form of pocket money, but this is gradually withdrawn as young
people grow up and start earning their own incomes, perhaps from
Saturday jobs or other part-time work (Jamieson and Corr, 1990). This
they can do legally from the age of 13 in Britain, and around half of
the National Child Development Study (NCDS) birth cohort had part-
time paid jobs at 16 years (Jones, 1986), and one-third of those interviewed more recently for the ESRC 16–19 Initiative (Jamieson and
Corr, 1990). It has been suggested that while many middle-class children are encouraged by their parents to have a Saturday job because it
is good for them to be self-reliant, for the children of working-class
families, part-time working may have a more material meaning (Jamieson and Corr, 1990; Hutson and Cheung, 1991). Young people in
poorer families may draw less on household resources if they have an
income from part-time work (MacLennan *et al.*, 1985).

Financial help further decreases as young people leave education
and enter the formal labour market. Analysis of the Scottish Young
People's Survey (SYPS) (see below) longitudinal data suggests that
while most (around two-thirds) young people were receiving money
from their parents at 17 years in 1987, the proportion decreased with
age, so that by the time the cohort was aged 19, only a minority were
still receiving financial help from their parents. These consisted mainly of young people still in full-time education and children of middle-
class families (Jones, 1992). Financial dependence on parents tends
therefore to be more protracted among the middle class (and indeed
as Bell, 1968, indicated, continues beyond the time that middle-class
young adults have left their parents' homes). Financial dependence
on parents throughout the teenage years is, however, an exception
rather than the rule for most young people.

Apart from money, parents may provide for their children with
gifts, often of a very practical nature, such as clothes. Wallace (1987b)
has indicated that as young people get older, they are less likely to
receive pocket money from their parents and more likely to receive
indirect support, in the form of food, clothing or cigarettes. Young
people living in rural areas sometimes had parental help in buying

their own cars, and thus improving their access to work and leisure (Wallace *et al.*, 1991a). Jamieson and Corr (1990) have also reported a loan from parents for this purpose. Corrigan (1989), has suggested that in the case of mother–daughter relationships, the opposite process may occur, and clothing transactions may be replaced with money gifts, as daughters become older and want to assert more individuality of style. Father–son relationships may also involve a particular form of financial exchange, as Bell (1968) has indicated.

These transactions can be complex. There is complexity associated with particular statuses: Allatt and Yeandle (1986) speak of the 'tightrope' that parents may have to tread between trying to protect their unemployed son or daughter (by helping with money) and trying to force them into work (by withholding it). There is also the complexity associated with change: Jamieson and Corr (1990) report a case where a girl who had been receiving pocket money took on a part-time job, and her pocket money was stopped. When she gave up this job, she did not go back onto pocket money again, but started to receive payment for jobs done around the house. From our own interpretation, it seems that she had passed a status threshold and could not therefore retrace her steps. The case emphasizes the importance of the *process* of economic independence.

Board money

Whereas in the United States, young people seldom pay any contribution to their parents when they are living in the parental home, except when the parents' financial situation becomes desperate (Coleman, 1986, quoted in Morris, 1990), in Britain, board money is not the exception, but the rule. It is a practice which brings abruptly into question the assumption of dependence in youth.

The payment of board money by children living in their parents' homes has long been a common practice, and shows no signs of discontinuing. It seems though that, following Millward (1968) and recent research (Hutson and Jenkins, 1987; Wallace, 1987b; Jamieson and Corr, 1990) that there has been a change in procedure in the last few decades. Previously, young workers would hand over their entire wage packets to their parents, and would receive pocket money in return (Carter, 1962); now, it is more common for young people to pay a fixed amount for their board and to retain control over the money they earn. This suggests a trend towards greater emancipation and financial control in youth; it seems to parallel the increased degree of financial control over the household budget experienced by married women in recent decades (Pahl, 1983, 1989). In other words, family finances are to a greater extent now controlled by individual family members, rather than by the father as head of household.

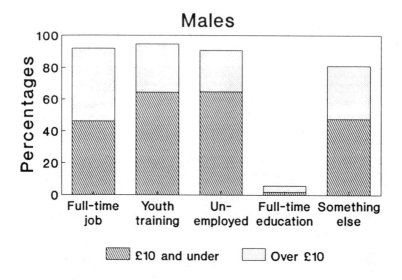

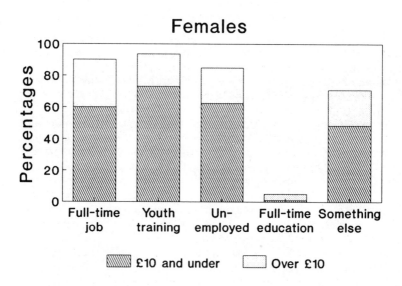

Figure 4.1 Paying board at 17 years by sex and economic status
Source: Scottish Young People's Survey, 1985 (Jones, 1992).

The amounts paid in board do not represent the true value of the accommodation, food and domestic services provided by parents to their children – amounts of £10, £15 or £20 are the most common (see Jones, 1991a) – and this has led some writers to consider the payment of board money in educational terms, or associated with moral issues of responsibility (Hutson and Jenkins, 1987). Hayes (1991) has shown the importance of the moral dimension of parent–child exchanges, including families where unemployment was not a factor. Similarly, Wallace (1987b) found that parents, though they expected board money, thought of it as a means of keeping a young person 'straight', rather than as a realistic sum. Allatt and Yeandle (1986) report that a 'concept of fairness' is applied by different families in different ways: in one family siblings may end up paying the same amount; while in another, graduated rates would be paid according to income.

Figure 4.1 is also based on data from the SYPS. The survey took place in 1985, when the cohort was aged around 17, and shows patterns of paying board money by economic status and sex. On leaving full-time education, young people begin to pay their parents towards the cost of their keep, and as we shall show, begin to free themselves from parental control. There is a sharp division, clearly shown in this chart, between those in full-time education and those in the labour market, whether employed, on training schemes, or unemployed.

The amount paid, according to Figure 4.1, depends on several factors. It depends on a young person's own economic circumstances (for example, though they still pay, those on training schemes or unemployed pay less than those with jobs – a pattern which we assume relates to the incomes associated with these positions). It is important to note that traineeship and unemployment (unlike full-time education) did not bring dispensation, but survey data may not bring out the full complexity of this issue. For example, in their South Wales study, Hutson and Jenkins (1987) found that the parents of unemployed young people insisted on their paying board money, so that they at least gave the appearance of 'paying their way', but they then found discrete ways of returning the money to avoid hardship. Survey data which measures one aspect of the financial relationship between parents and children therefore has its limitations. On the other hand, it does show systematic variation.

The amount of board money paid also, according to the SYPS, appears to depend on the economic circumstances of the family. In poorer families, measured by the employment status of the father, the presence of a lone mother, lower social class and larger families, young people paid more towards their board, thus contributing a larger proportion of the household income. Because the amount paid may be low in absolute terms, it is too easy to dismiss a young person's contribution on the grounds that it hardly covers the cost of their food, let alone reflects the true cost of their keep; this would be to deny two important facts – first, the amount may represent a sizeable chunk of a young person's income and secondly it might represent in poor families a more than sizeable chunk of the household income (Jones, 1991a, 1992).

It is curious therefore that wages legislation and recent social security changes have overlooked the financial contributions that young people make. As Roberts and his colleagues (1986: 29) pointed out:

> It seems to have been tacitly assumed that 16–18 year olds who live with their parents have minimum income needs and domestic responsibilities, and therefore will suffer no harm if their wages are forced down.

Contrary to policy expectations, described in Chapter 3, it seems that unemployment and low income in youth do not necessarily increase a young person's dependence on their families. The degree of dependence also relates to their families' economic circumstances.

Work in the home

The work young people do around the home may also have an important economic significance. According to Jamieson (1986) young people have been regarded over the decades as a reserve of domestic labour. There are indications that domestic work may involve payment, dispensation from board money, or other economic reward (see, for example, Jamieson and Corr, 1990; Jones, 1991a).

The domestic tasks done by young people in their parents' homes vary by gender, so that more cleaning work and child care (such as baby-sitting) is done by young women and more (though only slightly more) gardening and decorating done by young men (Griffin, 1985; Wallace, 1987a; Jones, 1992). Wallace (1987b) found that while daughters paid less board money than sons, they made up the deficit through housework, as a payment in kind. Research by Jones (1992) on the SYPS suggests a more complex picture, indicating that it was only middle-class daughters who could consider housework as a board payment in kind; working-class daughters had the double burden of domestic work and board money.

One result of gender socialization in the home, through gendered allocation of domestic tasks, is that young women learn to care for themselves (cooking, cleaning, laundry and so on) while living with their parents, and are thus better prepared for independent living when they eventually leave their parents' homes. This is reflected in the types of homes they move into, as Chapter 5 will show. Sons tend to remain physically dependent on their parents, mainly their mothers (who do their cooking and washing) for longer.

CHANGING ECONOMIC AND POWER RELATIONSHIPS

The discussion so far has shown that in considering the family as an economic unit, the changing roles of all its members should be taken into account. Figure 4.2, still based on the SYPS, shows in purely financial terms how the economic relationship between young people and their parents changes from a situation where the child is dependent on the parent for his or her income, which comes in the form of pocket money, to a situation where the 'child' becomes more and more economically independent of the parents, through an income from work or state benefits (though since the changes in social security regulations in 1988, eligibility for the latter has become problematic). This process of transition to economic adulthood starts while young people are living with their parents. At the age of 17, the general flow of cash payments is from parent to child; by the age of 19, the general flow is the other way, from child to parent in the form

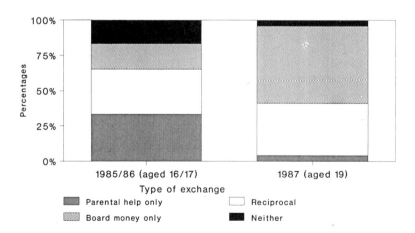

Figure 4.2 Parent–child financial exchanges among those at home and in the labour force

Source: Scottish Young Peoples' Survey 1985/6/7 (Jones, 1992).

of board money, at least among those who are living at home and not in full-time education. The findings indicate a degree of inter-dependence in parent–child relations (albeit within a power im-balance) and elements of 'short-term reciprocity' (Jones, 1992), which we do not usually associate with youth. Hutson and Jenkins (1987) have similarly commented on economic transfers in both directions between young people and their parents.

Growing up in a family also involves changes in the power relations within families. Many of these changes have an economic basis: it is by taking on economic roles that children start on the road to adult independence, and become emancipated from parental control. The moment children start earning, even from a Saturday job, their de-pendence on their parents begins to decrease and their power in their family to increase. As Allatt and Yeandle (1986: 21) pointed out, earn-ing brings the ability to contribute to the household income and to buy gifts: 'Income allows the individual to be generous ... Giving confers power upon the giver.' The ability to contribute board money to the household brings with it some new freedoms, such as sanction to stay out later at night, or to have more freedom in spending. Willis (1984: 19) describes the importance to young men of the wage as 'the golden key', giving protection from 'the aggression and exploitation of work, from the patriarchal dependencies of the parental home'.

Adolescence thus becomes a phase of considerable ambiguity, in-volving some delicate negotiation between children and their par-ents, especially in re-constituted families containing step-parents and step-siblings. Other work on parent–child relations, from the News-ons' (1976) study of 7-year-olds to more recent work on young people's relationships with their families (Allatt and Yeandle, 1986; Hutson and Jenkins, 1989) has stressed the extent to which roles and relationships are continually negotiated and changing. There are ad-justments in relation to other siblings, as young people grow up, for example, as they leave full-time education, and as family circum-stances change, for example if parents become unemployed.

As Pat Allatt has indicated (1986: 14), negotiations are taking place between young people and other family members too, not just their parents:

> For the majority of young people, therefore, independence un-folds in the home within an established pattern of family rela-tionship. For independence to be finally achieved, however, these relationships must be renegotiated. The mere facts of a child reaching certain ages and leaving school are recognized by par-ents and children as heralding changes in the relationship be-tween the generations; but paid employment endows the young adult with added power when negotiating rights, duties, obliga-tions and reciprocities with parents and siblings.

Pocket money and financial transfers provide an example. There are no hard and fast rules about how much pocket money parents should give their children. Allatt and Yeandle (1986) show the difficulty that parents face in trying to do the right thing – according to a 'concept of fairness', and in order to allow the young to gain increasing independence. The aim is to achieve what commentators have described as a delicate balance (Leonard, 1980; Finch, 1989) in the relationships between parents and their children. Becoming an adult involves negotiations such as these and they are part of the process of movement from dependence to independence, though the distinction between the two states is necessarily blurred (Finch, 1989; Jones, 1992). Even when young people leave home, their relations with their parents retain some of this complexity and ambivalence (Finch, 1989: 169):

It appears that the desired relationship is a very subtle blend of dependence and independence which people often regard as quite difficult to accomplish successfully, although they have a fairly clear idea of what they are aiming for.

Throughout the adolescent period, there is in the parent–child relationship a tension between the parent's desire to keep their children dependent and to allow them to grow into independent adults. This is also reflected in Diana Leonard's (1980) description of the strategy adopted by some parents of 'spoiling' young people who had left home and thus maintaining an element of dependence, as a way of reconciling such tensions. Hutson and Jenkins similarly identify two parental dilemmas of choice and conscience, in families where young people are unemployed. Their findings (Hutson and Jenkins, 1987: 23) echo those of Allatt and Yeandle, as well as Leonard's:

First, we found a conflict between, on the one hand, attempting to cushion one's offspring against the hardship of unemployment and, on the other, not wanting to make things *too* comfortable for them, at the expense of teaching them the proper value of money. Second, there is also the contradiction between giving young people their independence whilst, at the same time, 'keeping an eye'. It is not, perhaps, surprising that some mothers blamed their son's or daughter's unemployment on their own mis-handling of these values.

These tensions must be at their peak when young people are becoming economically independent adults but still living at home with their parents. We have spoken above of the move towards reciprocity in parent–child economic relations, of circumstances in which young people are important providers to the household and of parents' ambivalence about allowing their children to grow up. We have talked of the gradual shift in power relations as young people take more responsibility for themselves and depend less on the authority of their parents. It should perhaps not be forgotten that as young people are growing up and experiencing the problems of transition to adulthood, their parents are likely to be entering middle age. As parents give up their responsibility for their young, they are likely simultaneously to be taking on responsibility for the older generation of their own parents. The shifts in family relationships are likely to be stressful for everyone (and state policies should therefore take care not to upset delicate balances).

DEPENDENT CHILDREN?

There is a close association between economic transitions and the acquisition of rights and responsibilities. Access to an independent income allows a young person to buy rights in the domestic sphere and become more emancipated from parental control; but it also means that they have to take increasing responsibility for their own finances, and will lose their right to pocket money (which is associated with childhood and dependency). Emancipation thus comes at a price.

The transition to economic independence – in terms of family responsibilities and rights – is well under way in many cases not just prior to marriage but before a young person moves out of their parents' home. This contrasts with policy assumptions about the dependence of young people on their parents when living in the same household. Employment and training policies provide young people with 'component wages' (to use the terminology of Siltanen, 1986) rather than full adult wages; social security policies take no account of young people's financial responsibilities, when they are living at home. Yet in practice it is possible (see for example, Allatt, 1986) for young people's incomes to be crucial to family economies, to an extent that, in some cases, far from young people being dependent on their parents, sometimes their parents are dependent on them.

Unfortunately, though they may be trying to negotiate increased freedom from parental control during this stage, young people get little support from the state. In social security legislation, the right of access to subsistence levels of social security has over the last decade been increasingly withdrawn from young people (Roll, 1990; see Chapter 3). Families in all social groups are increasingly forced to behave according to the middle-class norms we have seen, and extend their financial responsibilities towards their young. Those under 18 are now forced into dependence on their parents if they cannot find

employment: if they are unemployed, they cannot claim unemployment benefit, and if they are on training schemes, their training allowances assume the availability of continued parental support. Even
young adults are expected to be able to continue their dependence on
their parents. Though the age of legal majority (and access to political
citizenship rights) in Britain is 18 years, young adults from 18 to 25
years are not entitled to full adult rates of social security, or often of
adult wages, and therefore do not attain social citizenship at this
stage.

All this represents a form of social control through enforced dependency, currently enacted through the social security regulations and
to be extended through the Criminal Justice Bill (which seeks to make
parents responsible for their children's fines). Parental support and
parental control are thus more forcibly linked in the policy sphere.
The twin policy needs – to cut social security costs and to stress 'law
and order' issues – are fulfilled by making children dependent on their
parents and consequently under their parents' control, all as Marsland has advocated (1986). In such circumstances, emancipation
from family and state control is dependent on employment.

The concept of emancipation is, however, problematic when applied to young people. Parsons (1956) pointed out how families must
help in emancipating the child from dependency (Parsons, 1956: 19);
Beck (1987) speaks of forcible emancipation of the young person
within the family; Harris (1983) suggests that emancipation from parental control may result from the transition into an independent
household (a point explored in Chapter 5). Economic dependency is
associated with being controlled; economic independence is associated with autonomy and freedom.

In the case of young people, are emancipation and independence to
be fought for or should they be conferred? Giddens refers to eman-
cipatory politics as the attempt to overcome illegitimate domination
as concerned with exploitation, inequality and oppression (Giddens
1991: 211). There have indeed been movements aimed to prevent the
exploitation of children and young people – though generally these
movements are not run by young people themselves, but by adults,
on their behalf. The Children's Rights movement of this century, the
nineteenth-century movements against child labour and cruelty to
children, are all of this kind. In the present day, the main pressure
group pressing for young people's rights has been Youthaid. Because
of their dependency on adults and domination by adults, and because
of their heterogeneity, children and young people are unable to take
up the cudgels on their own behalf. Yet their domination is not necessarily illegitimate, nor is their dependency – both are essential to
parental care and control of *a child*. It is in the period of *youth* that the

conflict is set up, when the dependent child is becoming the independent adult. Emancipation on an individual level can be fought for and won within the family, but at a societal level young people have no real power to claim rights as a social group. Rights and responsibilities in youth are imposed from above.

There is, however, a basic ambiguity – emancipation and citizenship status derive from economic independence, but some recognition of emancipation and access to some citizenship rights are required for the achievement of economic independence. This creates a 'double-bind' to which many young people are subject as they become older.

5

INDEPENDENCE FROM

THEIR FAMILIES?

Some transitions to independence can occur while young people are still living with their families, as Chapter 4 showed, but for most, the first and perhaps most symbolic step towards independence is taken when they leave their parents' homes and begin to establish homes of their own. In this chapter we shall examine the extent to which leaving home does represent emancipation and independence, and also identify ways in which the whole process of household and family formation may be structured by pressures emanating from the family which is being left, the inequalities of the market and the policies of the state.

The process of leaving home takes place at the junction between the public and private worlds of young people – in leaving home they are leaving the private world of family relations and encountering the public world and formal relations of housing markets, labour markets, and other adult institutions. The changes occur at the heart of the transition from dependent child to independent adult. And so, leaving home and household formation are associated with other transitions, such as those associated with family formation, post-school education, or entry into the labour market (see also Bloss *et al.*, 1990). These transitions may even be interdependent.

We shall consider here the transitions to adulthood relating to household and family formation. First we will examine how these transitions have changed over time, and we will illustrate the difficulty of arriving at any simple definition of adulthood. Our aim is to examine the significance of leaving home as a transition step. Secondly we will use empirical research to examine more closely the relationship between leaving home and emancipation. We bring together some of the themes associated with citizenship in youth earlier, looking at the relationship between civil, political and social rights in youth, as well as access to them, and further question some of the assumptions about dependence and independence which underlie policies structuring economic status and direct access to citizenship rights.

CHANGING PATTERNS OF TRANSITION

The relationship between starting work, leaving the parental home, getting married and the attainment of adult status is complex, and appears to have altered over time. Research by social historians and demographers in Britain suggests that the relationship between leaving home and forming marital partnerships in particular has changed. It is important therefore to re-evaluate the significance of these events in the attainment of adult status.

Over time, the nature of each pathway in the transition to adulthood has changed, both in its timing and in its nature. The relationship between paths of transition, such as that between employment careers and family formation, or that between family formation and household formation, has also changed, particularly in terms of the timing of transitions and thus the spacing between them. This is largely because the structures affecting individual transitions have changed. We have considered the changing structures affecting economic status and access to an income – the structures of education, employment and training (Chapter 2), and the structures of the social security system (Chapter 3). In Chapter 4, we considered the changes that have occurred in family structures, which also affect patterns of becoming adult, forcing us to reconsider our assumptions about family life. As we have already said, it is important to incorporate both structure and process in the study of youth.

Social historians have shown that the relationship between the various strands in the transition to adulthood, and their timing and spacing, varies over time. The time relationship between starting work, leaving home, getting married and having children, among those who do all of these things, has changed in particular. Indeed Gillis (1985) has described the changing shape of the general pattern over time as that of an hour glass (see Figure 5.1), with wide spacing between the different transition elements in the nineteenth and early twentieth centuries, narrowing (and indeed at their most connected) in the middle period at the middle of the twentieth century, and now widening (and becoming less connected) again as the millennium reaches its close. Within this framework, there has been change in the significance of each of the events involved in the transition to adult-

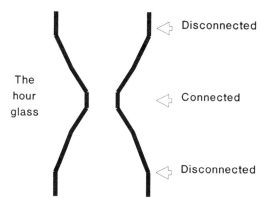

Figure 5.1   Connected or disconnected transitions?

hood. Our discussion of developments in the sociology of youth in Chapter 1 showed how theories have changed over time. In practice, concepts of youth and transition have reflected the historical age in which they were formulated – when transitions were at their most connected, the functionalists were developing theories of socialization based on unitary transition; with the increased diversity and complexity of transitions in recent years, and the loosening of their connection, more post-modernist ideas of youth have begun to find support.

Attaining adult status

The more complex the transitions to adulthood become and the looser the connection between them, the more difficult it is to define the attainment of adult status. Figure 5.2 provides a framework within which to consider changes in the nature of leaving home, household formation and family formation over time. In pre-industrial times, children from the age of 10 frequently left the homes of their parents to take up positions as living-in servants in other households; they may then have spent 15 years or so in this surrogate household before marrying and forming households of their own (Laslett, 1971). In the mid-nineteenth century too, though young people in the higher social classes stayed longer in their parental homes, working-class young people often left home in adolescence to live in another household as servants or apprentices, or moved from rural villages to board with families in towns (Anderson, 1971, 1983; Wall, 1978). For many young people throughout this period, there was an intermediate

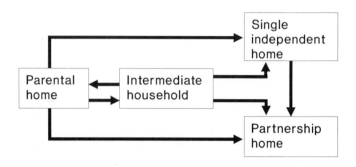

Figure 5.2   Household formation transitions

household situation between living as a dependent child in the family home and living as an independent adult in a 'marital' home. This acted, perhaps, as a buffer between childhood and adulthood. The act of leaving home was thus not associated *per se* with the attainment of adult status: this was gained mainly through marriage and parenthood.

By the middle of the twentieth century, there had been many changes, including particularly a contraction of the time span between leaving home and getting married (Anderson, 1983). Transitions reached their most connected stage (the narrowest part of the 'hour glass'). Functionalist sociologists such as Parsons and Coleman, writing mainly in the 1950s and 1960s, describe a normative and unitary transition to adulthood, and indeed their work appears to have coincided with a period in history when transitions were at their most condensed and connected. The functionalist theories had posited that reproduction of social institutions such as the family, the labour force, and the social class structure all formed one cyclical process of social reproduction (Willis, 1977; Aggleton, 1987; Wallace, 1987a). New adult members of society were 'inserted' with the appropriate training and expectations: thus education produced workers; work produced a particular model of family life; and in its turn this model of the family was associated with particular forms of consumption and gender roles.

During the early post-war period, leaving home had indeed become more associated with marriage, to the extent that social scientists could use age at marriage as a proxy variable for age at leaving home (as Young, 1984, in Australia, and Kiernan, 1985, in Britain, have both pointed out). This was due to several factors, including the increase in minimum age at leaving education, the greater numbers going on to further and higher education, the lowering (at the time) of the age at marriage (Kiernan, 1983, 1985), and the availability of relatively cheap rented accommodation. In consequence, because of its greater association with marriage and parenthood, leaving home had become more significant in the attainment of adult status.

The transitions have become more extended, more spaced and more complex in recent years – the widening of the 'hour glass'. Unemployment rose with the economic recession and decline in the manufacturing industry in the 1970s, and young school leavers were increasingly likely to enter training schemes rather than employment. The nature of family formation transitions also changed, with the 'sexual revolution' of the 1960s and with more knowledge about, and access to, contraceptives. Household transitions were affected by the contraction of the housing market and high inflation increased the availability and cost of 'first homes'. The result was a change in the very nature of the 'marital' home: the age at first marriage rose, more couples delayed childbirth, more cohabited (often as a prelude to marriage), and more were forming homosexual partnerships. This is by no means an exhaustive list, either of causes or effects, but it serves to show that the normative patterns of transition, such as those described by Parsons, had become weaker. Some writers questioned the universality of transitions to adulthood. Paul Willis (1984), for example, warned that youth unemployment impeded the process of becoming adult. Other writers took a more moderate view and suggested that patterns of transition were adapted rather than disrupted as a result of unemployment during youth (Wallace, 1987a; Hutson and Jenkins, 1989). Thus it has been suggested that young women with experience of unemployment may be more likely than those without such experience to become mothers in their teenage years (Phoenix, 1991). There is some association between fertility and unemployment among young men, as well, though the nature of the link is unclear (Payne, 1989).

Family formation

In Chapter 4, some of the recent changes in family structure resulting from family dissolution were discussed. There have also, and indeed perhaps in consequence, been some important recent trends in family formation, as Kiernan and Wicks (1990) have shown. Cohabitation among young people has become more common, so that there are fewer marriages involving young people and the age at marriage is rising. The proportion of all marriages involving teenage brides halved between 1980 and 1987. The median age at first marriage rose from 21.4 years in 1971, to 21.8 years in 1980 and to 23.3 years in

1987. Kiernan and Wicks show that there are more single women and more cohabiting couples, *vis-à-vis* married couples, among young adults now, and 'it is virtually a majority practice to cohabit before marrying' (Kiernan and Wicks, 1990: 8).

Nevertheless, as Mansfield and Collard point out (1988: 199), most people do still marry at some stage in their lives. It is the significance of marriage which has changed, and possibly diminished. The young man who unwittingly provided these authors with the title of their book may be representing an increasingly minority view:

> Getting married is where it all starts. You're not a kid any more, you're branching out on your own. *It's the beginning of the rest of your life.* [our emphasis].

With the increased rate of divorce and breakdown of marriages, a first marriage may thus represent another stage in life. Just as Mansfield and Collard found that the route taken into marriage was often a fairly 'haphazard trail', so might the route out of it.

The increase in cohabitation in the 1980s meant that there was an increased separation of marriage and childbearing. The median age at first birth among women has increased, from 24 years in 1970, to 26.5 years in 1987 (Kiernan and Wicks, 1990). Two-thirds of births to women under 25 years were extra-marital in 1988, but at the same time, more and more children born outside marriage were being registered by both parents, rather than just by the mother, and in more and more cases, the two registering parents were cohabiting (Kiernan and Wicks, 1990). This suggests that the nature of cohabiting relationships is changing, in particular with respect to the responsibility of fathers. Despite these indications that cohabitation is becoming both more socially acceptable and incorporating much of the ideology of married family life, there has been much Government concern about apparent collapsing moral standards among parents, and attempts to place more responsibility on them.

Equally, some of the 'moral panic' about teenage pregnancy appears to surround the notion that young women may get pregnant in order to jump housing queues, obtain welfare benefits and so on. Even Willis (1984: 13) suggests that high levels of unemployment may have the following consequence:

> The disappearance of the role of the male as future breadwinner may fundamentally alter the sexual and romantic relations between the sexes. If you can't escape from home through the earning power of a young man, an alternative way to 'get your own place' may simply be to become pregnant and rely on the state to house and support you.

There appears to be no evidence, however, that supports the notion that getting pregnant may represent a housing strategy (Greve and

Currie, 1990), though early pregnancy and homelessness may present themselves simultaneously, both being affected by other factors. Other research has also shown that there is no reason to believe that teenage mothers make 'worse' parents than older ones. Yet despite the lack of evidence, moral panics abound (Phoenix, 1991) and teenage mothers may feel in consequence very unsupported (Sharpe 1987).

Household formation

Recent research also suggests some further changes in the patterns of household formation, indicating that the significance of leaving home could be changing once more. It has become more common for young people, either alone or with peers, to set up single independent households which are neither associated with a partnership, nor part of an intermediate household situation (such as where people leaving home join an existing household). The development of individual or peer group independent households may well be a new phenomenon, though, as we shall see, the old patterns do still exist alongside the new. The implication, though, may be that, as Harris (1983: 221) has suggested, young adults may now no longer depend on marriage and/ or parenthood for adult status: they may now be *emancipated* from parental control and define themselves as independent prior to marriage (see also Bloss *et al.*, 1990; Galland, 1990). For many women, this could involve a period of emancipation between dependent childhood and the further economic dependency which is likely to be associated with marriage and parenthood. After all, by becoming householders, young people should be in a position of power in the market-place, and able to participate fully as citizens in the society in which they thus become located. We shall see if this is the case.

VARIATION IN TRANSITIONS TO ADULTHOOD

Apart from variation across time, the picture is made more complex because of the systematic variation in patterns of transition across social groups. We have already seen in Chapter 4 that in economic terms, becoming an adult is a process which is differentiated between social groups. This is also the case with the timing and spacing of events relating to the transition to adulthood. Here we draw on studies which have been more fully reported elsewhere (see Jones, 1987b, 1990a). First, we shall show findings from the National Child Development Study, a national birth cohort last surveyed in 1981 at the age of 23 years, and the General Household Survey (GHS). The findings relate to the period around 1980, prior to the many policy changes of the Conservative Government which came to power in 1979, to the period of widespread youth unemployment, to the introduction of training schemes to fill the increasing gap between school and work, and to a great extent prior to the major contraction of the rented housing market – all factors which were later to affect patterns of transition.

Figure 5.3 shows variation by social class and gender in the timing and spacing of transitions to adulthood, in terms of the median ages at which transition events occurred. The diagram is a schematic representation. Marriage here includes cohabiting partnerships or 'living as married'. The figure shows clearly that the working class leave full-time education (E), start work (W), marry or cohabit (M) and have children (C) before the middle class. Women marry or cohabit and have children before men, and in consequence, heterosexual partnerships tend to contain male partners who are on average two years older than females. The figure shows how the spacing of transitions varies, as well as their timing. While the spacing between leaving full-time education (E) and starting to live as married (M) remains stable across classes, it varies by gender, so that the average time span between the two transitions at the time of these surveys, was seven years for men and four years for women. This would seem to suggest that

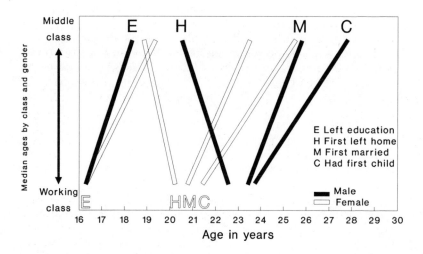

Figure 5.3   Transition events in youth
Source: Jones, 1988 (Figure 4).

full-time education at college or university actually defers the attainment of adulthood in Britain, at least in these terms. It is unusual for students (other than 'mature students') in Britain to have stable partnerships or children (in contrast to the situation in the United States, where marriage among students is common – according to Kerckhoff, 1990). Education thus acts as an important intervening variable between social class and transition outcome, structuring the timing of marriage or cohabitation.

Gender differences, on the other hand, are highlighted in Figure 5.3: men have longer in the labour force than women, before forming partnerships. The mechanisms which cause this age disparity in many partnerships have never clearly been identified, but are probably a reflection of other gender disparities, such as in occupational structures and career opportunities, as well as in the degree of socialization into future gender roles which takes place during life within the family of origin. Next, Figure 5.3 shows that some direct social class effects do prevail: the household and family formation transitions (H, M and C) are far less closely connected among the middle class than among the working class. Furthermore, marriage (or cohabiting partnership) and childbirth occur at an earlier age among the working class than among the middle class, as Wallace (1987a) has also shown. Finally, it indicates that leaving home (H) is more associated with family formation among the working class than among the middle class.

Any attempt to understand the significance of these different life events in the attainment of adulthood therefore needs to account for these social class and gender differences. There are also likely to be further variations according to disability (following Clark and Hirst, 1989) and according to ethnic group – but these will be complex, and are not in any case visible in these data sets. In terms of social class and gender differences, however, we are left with a question. Why do the more socially disadvantaged (women and the working class) become 'adult', in these terms, sooner than the more advantaged social groups?

WHAT DOES 'ADULT STATUS' MEAN?

Definitions of adulthood tend to come from social psychology and tend to indicate varying numbers of stages through which young people are assumed to pass (such as leaving school, starting a job, courtship, leaving home, getting married, having children, etc.) though increasingly in practice not all people follow these mapped-out paths: some stages are missed – parenthood can precede marriage, paths may reverse – those who have left home can return to their parents to live, yet people still become identifiably adult. When family structures can be diverse, and relationships complex, as Chapter 4 has shown, how can we identify an individual's location in one family or household form with adult independence, and in another with childhood dependence? So what does adult status mean? Can it be achieved through setting up an independent home, or through marriage and parenthood, for example, without reference to economic and social status, to physical maturity or to legal recognition of adult citizenship?

Wallace has suggested that in lieu of the 'rites of passage' which mark the attainment of adult status in pre-industrial societies, we now have 'markers' of status, which can be determined and ratified *privately, publicly* or *officially*. Private markers, may be very private indeed, such as a first sexual experience, or first alcoholic drink, which though not necessarily ratified by others, nevertheless may be a significant status 'gain'; public markers may include engagement parties, weddings, and so on, primarily drawing recognition from the family or the community; official markers might include certificates for qualifications, or the right to draw unemployment benefit, or the granting of a mortgage. The important point is that adult status may have different meanings in the private, public and official spheres, but may require recognition in each sphere.

Indeed, adulthood as a concept seems to be such a mixture of physical attribute, age, and economic, social or legal definition, as to be meaningless. Becoming an adult, in terms of reaching the legal age of majority (currently 18 years, in Britain), is decreasing in its significance, since it no longer brings the rights to welfare provision once associated with adult status (see Chapter 3). A look at the ages at which the rights and responsibilities associated with adult status and citizenship are officially achieved (see Table 5.1 for a rough guide), makes us wonder on what basis, other than arbitrary, these laws and regulations were created. It seems that different sets of guidelines underlie different sets of rules.

As a result of some of these (in our view) arbitrary sets of rules – arbitrary in the way that they fix on physical age without reference to the individual life course, the period of youth has for some young people and in some spheres been formally extended quite drastically in recent years in Britain. As we saw in Chapter 3, state welfare policies since 1979 are increasingly taking responsibility for the young from the state and attempting to transfer it onto their families. Welfare benefits have become increasingly age-graded, and the age of dependency has been increased: the age of entitlement to some welfare benefits is now 25. This has made it more difficult for young people under that age to leave home and successfully maintain an independent household, unless they or their partners have steady,

Table 5.1 Transition ages in legislation

Age	Legislation
10	Age of criminal responsibility (8 in Scotland)
13	Child employment minimum age
16	Leave school
	Age of consent (heterosexual)
	Drive motor scooter
	Marry with parents' consent
17	Adult jurisdiction
	Drive car
18	Age of majority
	Sign tenancy (16 in Scotland)
	Drink alcohol
	Claim unemployment benefit
	Claim social security
21	Previous age of majority
	Legal homosexuality (male)
25	Adult levels of Income Support
26	Adult in housing benefit rules

secure and well-paid employment, and the median age at first leaving home may rise as a result. The transition to adulthood is now structured by access to employment to a greater extent than before.

There are clearly problems with definitions of adulthood. Highlighting the problems of definition, some writers, particularly in France and Germany, have started talking of 'post-adolescence' as a newly-emerged stage of the life course characterized by the extension of education and extended dependency on parents beyond the age of 18 – and sometimes into the 30s (Zinnekar, 1981 in Germany; Galland, 1990, in France; Gaiser, 1991). The need to explain these developments through defining a new stage in the life course reflects the need for a cogent theory for explaining the process of youth and re-defining adulthood itself. In other words, the decreasing connectedness of transitions, their increasing diversity of form and their variability across social groups has resulted in the collapse of the whole theoretical framework (both 'vertical' in terms of structure and 'horizontal' in terms of process) for understanding adulthood, as well as youth.

What is it about adult status that makes its attainment desirable? We would argue that its desirability lies in the package of rights and responsibilities, in particular the right to full participation in society, which tends to be associated with adult status. How can we explain how economic status might structure the attainment of adult status, withholding it from those without jobs (as Willis, 1984, suggested)?

We suggest that though citizen's rights may be acquired with age, access to those rights is structured by economic status. Full participation in society is not necessarily associated with the traditional markers of adult status, marriage and parenthood. Indeed, marriage can create economic dependency among women and limit rather than increase their access to the rights of full citizenship. By seeing adulthood in terms of access to, as well as rights of, citizenship, we can overcome some of the conceptual difficulties, and can better understand why women and the working class, both disadvantaged groups, appear in traditional terms to achieve adult status first.

This, then, is the backcloth against which we need to understand the process of leaving home and the inequalities apparent in household formation. In Chapter 4, we showed that the transition to economic independence is enacted within the parent–child relationship in the private sphere of the parental home, and is associated with moves towards emancipation. It is important to look at patterns of leaving home in this context. Here we will question the degree of independence and emancipation which accompanies leaving home and household formation. We will show both ongoing inequalities in youth and new ways in which the state intervenes and further stratifies young people's lives. Developing our citizenship thesis further, we will consider whether leaving home marks the beginning of full participation in society.

INDEPENDENCE THROUGH LEAVING HOME

Is it important, as we have indicated, to recognize that the transition from dependence to independence starts while young people are living in their parental homes, or other homes of origin. This is not acknowledged in social security policies which are based on the assumption that young people can derive their rights as citizens from their parents, being dependent on them. If in practice young people cannot be seen to be dependent while living in their homes of origin, can they be described as independent when they move out of these homes? Leaving home represents the move from the private world of the family to the public world: issues of dependence and independence transfer more visibly from the family to the state. Does this move make their position *vis-à-vis* the state any less ambiguous?

At some stage in their lives, most people leave their parents' homes, sometimes in search of some privacy and freedom. Allan and Crow (1988) refer to young people who wanted a home of their own for privacy or control over their own space. The median age of leaving home (for the NCDS cohort) was 20 years for women and 21.9 years for men (Jones, 1987b) – i.e. considerably younger than the age of maturity now reflected in Government ideology and policies.

To what extent is leaving home to be associated with economic independence and emancipation from parental control? While in many instances this is the case, there are nevertheless a number of problems with making a direct association between the two. The first problem is that the act of leaving home is not necessarily a claim for emancipation (cf. Harris, 1983), and young people do not always set themselves up as independent householders when they move away from their parents' homes. The next problem is that young people often leave home not from choice, but because of a variety of con-straints. A third problem is that when they leave home, they do not all have access to housing. Finally, they do not always make a clean break with the home of origin – some may leave and return again, to leave for a second or third time at a later stage, while for others, the first move away from home may also be the final stage towards inde-pendent living. All these factors have to be taken into account, and we shall discuss each in turn, and consider their implications for social policy. Our focus here in on the types of households in which young people live on leaving home. The types of housing they enter, and their relationship with the housing market, are discussed in Chapter 6.

Independent and intermediate households

First, let us consider whether leaving home is a claim for indepen-dence. It is in practice hard to talk of changing patterns of household formation when so little research has been undertaken on this area of transition, but there does appear to have been an important and possibly significant change. It seems clear that young people are more likely to set up an independent household when they leave home, than probably ever before. This has been observed in France (Galland, 1990) and in Germany (Bloss *et al.*, 1990) as well as in Britain. Some-times, this means living in a single-person household; at other times, it means sharing with friends. There is also, however, occasionally an intermediate stage, in which some young people live with relatives other than their parents, or live in an institution such as a hostel, nurses' home, barracks and so on. The separation of the age of leaving home and the age at marriage does not necessarily therefore lead to increased independent living; nor does marriage necessarily mean household formation. Leaving home does not necessarily involve en-try into the housing market either as a tenant or buyer.

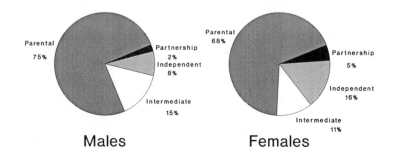

Figure 5.4　Households at 19 years
Source:　Scottish Young People's Survey, 1987.

Figure 5.4 shows the household circumstances of young people aged around 19 years in Scotland, according to data from the 1987 sweep of the Scottish Young People's Survey (SYPS). Household types are defined according to the typology shown in Figure 5.2. The figure shows that whatever new practices are occurring, it is still the case that many young people leaving home move into transitional intermediate households, which are analogous to the boarding or live-in servant situations of the nineteenth century. These intermediate household situations are sometimes associated with more transitional types of housing, such as hostels, which represent a very tentative entry into the housing market and may carry great risk of homelessness. Sometimes, they are associated with joining an existing household, for instance migration to towns and boarding with relatives in a manner very similar to that of the nineteenth century; or perhaps a young couple living with in-laws while waiting for a partnership home. Our data suggest that young people who have trouble finding housing may board with relatives as an expedient. Other examples are surrogate households, where young people move into student hostels or take up jobs which have housing attached, as in the armed forces (for men, especially from rural areas), nursing (for women), or the hotel industry – the security of these housing situations depends entirely on the security of the job, and in the case of hotel work which is often seasonal there may be particular risk. It is mainly younger people from working-class families and/or rural areas who are in these situations, and it is likely that they provide a teenager with the opportunity to leave home, though in many cases they also carry great risk. It is, perhaps, from these household situations that young people are most likely to return home to their parents to live, before leaving more permanently (and perhaps into more secure accommodation) later. These situations make us question the relationship between leaving home and emancipation, since the young people are still living in relatively dependent situations in many cases. These intermediate household situations still provide a half-way stage between status as a dependent non-householder, and a independent householder, just as they did in the past.

Next, we see marital and partnership households. Becoming a householder in Britain is still closely associated with marriage: most householders are marriage partners, and since women tend to form partnerships at a younger age than men, they also tend to become householders (or at least partners of) before men. Marriage partners and those living as married tend to be living in the most secure forms of accommodation, either in homes which they own or are buying, or in the shrinking public rented sector (Jones, 1987b). It is possible, however, that more young couples are now living with relatives because of the shortage of affordable housing. Households consisting of lone parents and their children – are also becoming more frequent, but are not shown up here because many young single parents still live with their own parents.

Finally, we also see more independent single households, either alone (own flat) or with peers (shared flat), as originally hypothesized. This, according to the GHS, occurs mainly among the middle class, including students (Jones, 1987b), and it suggests that many young people at least attempt to become emancipated prior to marriage (though it is important to remember that some people return home after they finish their course or job – a point we shall return to below). The proportion of independent single households seems to represent an interesting new development. Diana Leonard defined a 'home' very much in terms of a marital and family household (Leonard, 1980: 49):

> 'a home' is seen essentially as something which is developed by a married couple and their children ... To 'make a home' alone or with peers is a contradiction in folk terms and difficult in practice.

The existence of single independent households goes some way to challenge this view. At least, it suggests that young people may see the viability of a single-person household. However, the public, building societies and housing officials may not. Single independent households are associated with rented flats, more secure than hostels, and sometimes owned by at least one of the householders. Housing policies encouraging home ownership and withdrawing public-sector rented accommodation, together with the effects of the current recession and mortgage interest rates, could thus be forcing a decline in single independent living again.

According to Figure 5.4, men still appear to be dependent on others (usually women) for their physical needs, at the age of 19: working-class men are the most likely to move straight from parental home to partnership home, and male students are more likely to be in (supported) student accommodation than female students, who are more likely to be in shared flats (Jones, 1990a). This is to some extent an outcome of primary socialization and the gender division of labour in the family home: girls are more likely to do housework in the family, and thus more able to look after themselves in an independent housing situation, as Chapter 4 indicated.

Choice or constraint?

The second problem about associating leaving home with emancipation is that many people leave home not from choice, but precisely because they have no choice (we are here making an assumption that emancipation is associated with choice). The extent to which young people leave their parental homes because they want to is partly age-related.

The age at which people leave home and their reasons for leaving are closely linked (Figure 5.5, from NCDS data): at all ages, women tend to leave home mainly in order to live as married; among men, those aged over 20 leave mainly to marry, there is an exodus from the parental home at 18 years, of students leaving to go to college; younger home leavers do so in order to take up a job, or look for one, or because there are family problems. Thus it appears to be the case that the older people are when they leave home, the more likely they are to move straight into some form of partnership or single independent home. However, Figure 5.5 also shows that young people may be forced to leave home earlier, because of the need to find jobs or college places – reflecting inequalities in local job and education opportunities – or because of the financial circumstances in their families, or because of problems in family relationships, especially perhaps where there are step-families. These situations all appear to be associated with later homelessness (Greve and Currie, 1990; Liddiard and Hutson, 1991). In such circumstances, it is hard to identify leaving home with emancipation and adult status: there are clearly situations when young people leave home because they have to, rather than because they want to. When they are not necessarily able to choose the best time to leave, or the most favourable job and housing markets to move into, they become more susceptible to the risks of unemployment and homelessness.

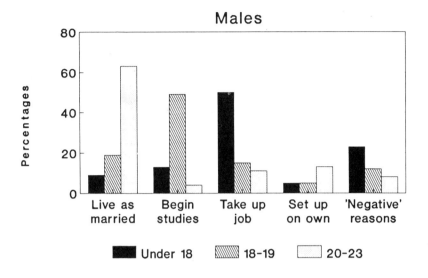

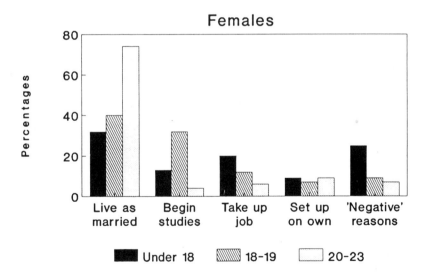

Figure 5.5 Reason for leaving home by age first left
Source: National Child Development Study, 1981 (Jones, 1987b).

Inequality of access to a home

The third problem of equating leaving home with emancipation lies in the inequality of access to housing (and thus households), again partly structured by age. Homelessness is the stark example of cases where leaving home and emancipation are not linked, and we deal with the issue in more detail in Chapter 6. Homelessness means in our view lack of access not just to a roof, but to a household (which may or may not include other people), to independent living, to space and to privacy. Homelessness is a growing social problem: it is growing at its fastest pace among those aged between 16 and 18, and more quickly among young adults generally than among those over 25 years (Randall, 1988). Agencies dealing with the homeless cannot cope with the increase in numbers. We increasingly see the evidence in the numbers of young people begging (with 'hungry and homeless' labels) on the city streets.

It has been suggested that around 30 per cent of young people who present as homeless to relief agencies have been in care at some stage, and it is likely that many of these became homeless on leaving care. The majority have, however, become homeless either on leaving their parental home or after some intermediate stage in the housing market. It seems likely that there are particular situations where lack of access to jobs, social security, housing, and family support may lead to homelessness.

The increase in homelessness among 16- and 17-year-olds is currently causing the most concern in Britain. In Scotland at least, this is not because of lack of a right to housing, since this age group has the right to sign a tenancy agreement (in contrast to the situation in England and Wales), or even necessarily because of a lack of access to housing (though appropriate housing is still a problem). The difficulty may result rather from the non-parallel development of citizenship rights referred to earlier (for discussion of how this operates at a societal level see Giddens, 1982; Turner, 1990). We argue that this needs to be acknowledged at an individual level too: while 16- and 17-year-olds have housing rights, they do not have the right to social security, and the lack of access in this one area of citizenship (social) affects access in another area (civil). Indeed there is often a further stage in this downward spiral, since homelessness often means that people are not on the electoral register and thus lose their political rights as well.

Returning home

Finally, there is the problem that young people do not necessarily make a clean break with their parents' home when they leave it. They may return to their parents again, and we shall be examining this practice below, and they may remain financially dependent on their parents even though they may not return home again – benefiting from gifts and money which may help them with the costs of home-building, for example. Bell (1968) has shown the importance of continued support from middle-class parents to their children after they have nominally broken free of economic dependence. Nor is parental help limited to the middle-class, as Harris (1983) has shown. Again, these practices should alert us to the danger of over-simplification when we speak of dependent children and independent adults.

Whether the process of leaving home has become less protracted, or whether it has simply changed in its nature and significance, is hard to determine. It has been suggested that the age of leaving home has recently risen. It may be that the process has been extended, so that the last leaving home event is later, while the age at first leaving home remains stable. There is as yet no evidence that the age at first leaving home has changed. What is clear, however, is that leaving home still often constitutes a process: leaving home is not necessarily a one-off event; people often leave and then return home, to leave again at a later stage. We do not know how often or over what period of time this may happen. The NCDS showed (Jones, 1987b) that of those currently living with their parents at 23 years, around one-third had left home at some stage to live away. These findings show how important it is to study a process with longitudinal data. Studies of leaving home which use cross-sectional data tend to measure the most recent leaving home event, and thus overestimate the age at first leaving home. The SYPS only covers young people up to the age of 19, and so only shows part of the process of leaving home, but even by 19 years, many who had left home had returned again. Returners are often those who originally left home to study or to take up a job, or leaving because of problems at home, and the suggestion is that if someone loses their job, or finishes their study, or is reconciled with their family, they may go back home before making their next career move, while those leaving home in order to live as married are, not surprisingly, the least likely to return.

The practice of returning home also causes problems of definition: for example, students may feel that they have left home, yet still return to their parents for the vacations, and as a result, perceptions of whether or not a young person has left home may vary considerably between young people and their parents, as Young (1987) found. Many of those who leave home may thus still regard their family home as a safety net, or they may feel that they have not really left. Leaving home in order to set up home, as a single person or in a partnership, is relatively infrequently associated with returning home and appears to be a more positive affirmation of adulthood (Jones, 1987b; Bloss *et al.*, 1990). The distinction drawn by Leonard (1980) between 'leaving home' and 'living away from home', the latter being more associated with returns, may therefore still hold for many young people, particularly students, who frequently return to their parents not only after their course is finished, but often during the vacations too. Indeed patterns of leaving home may change significantly among the student population, with the recent withdrawal of their housing benefit and benefit entitlement during the vacations. They in particular may be more likely to seek local courses so that they can remain at home, or become more dependent on returning home during the vacations.

Though the reason for leaving home may determine to some extent whether a young person is likely to return home, there are other, perhaps more important, determinants of patterns of leaving home. These include changes in the young person's economic circumstances, and the economic circumstances of their family of origin.

The 'safety nets' of the state and the family home

The Government response to youth homelessness has been to encourage young people to delay leaving home by withdrawing their social security entitlement so that they remain economically dependent on their parents and live in their parental homes, rather than by providing young people with realistic incomes and housing. The implication of this policy is that there is a correct age for leaving home, though this is not defined, and people who leave home below that age are not doing so for positive or practical reasons, but are running away. Indeed there has been an increasing tendency to refer to homeless young people as 'runaways', thus putting blame on them for their own condition. In seeking to deal with youth homelessness, the Government seems to have made the whole process of leaving home problematic. Although the median age of leaving home in Britain is around 21 years (Jones, 1987b), the state-recognized age of economic independence is considerably higher.

Whatever the prevailing class cultural practices associated with independence and household formation, it is no longer deemed appropriate in policy terms for young people under 25 years to make a 'successful' transition to full participation in society. Full participation below this age depends to a very great extent on an income from a steady and well-paid job; this effectively means that it depends on the local labour market, since leaving home to look for work is discouraged. Young people living in rural areas are particularly disadvantaged in this respect (but there is a question whether access to full social citizenship rights has ever been fully extended to the rural population, as the recent literature on rural deprivation would indicate – see Midwinter and Monaghan, 1990).

Since 1988, in an attempt to reduce the incidence of homelessness, state policies are now putting even more pressure on young people to delay their departure from the parental home, but these pressures may also be forcing young people to leave home earlier than they otherwise would; in other words, policies may be contributing to homelessness among the young, rather than reducing it. In order to understand how, it is first important to understand the patterns of economic exchanges described in Chapter 4. Young people pay board money to their parents, and pay more when their parents are poorer, including when their fathers are unemployed. Even in 1987, prior to the 1988 social security changes, it is apparent that young people with jobs were more likely to have left home by the age of 19 where their father was not in full-time employment. This would suggest that the increased responsibility of a young worker with an unemployed father to subsidize their families may in fact be a disincentive to staying at home. The housing benefit regulations (1984) may provide a further disincentive, since young workers are expected to pay a 'non-dependant rent contribution', which in many families may be over and above the amount they pay in board (and in addition also to the amount they currently pay in Poll Tax) (Jones, 1991a). Alternatively, the regulations can force a young person to stay at home for longer because of family responsibilities, as Claire Wallace's recent research seems to indicate.

State policy is also intended to encourage young people to return to their parental home if they become unemployed or risk homelessness. Indeed, recent SYPS surveys suggest an increase in the proportions returning home. But again, state policies can apparently misfire. The study previously quoted (Jones, 1991a) also shows that when young people who have left home become unemployed, they are far more likely to return to their parents' home if their fathers are employed than if their fathers are not in full-time work (in these circumstances, they are more likely to be able to be economically dependent on their families, and of course more likely to have access to information about local jobs). The recent changes in Income Support regulations described in Chapter 3 are likely to exacerbate this problem: if unemployed young people return home, they become the responsibility of their parents, who in many cases simply cannot afford to keep them.

Patterns of behaviour cannot necessarily be re-shaped by policies which are based on a static and homogeneous concept of youth. In other words, policies designed to overcome homelessness may in

practice be a cause of it. It is important to understand leaving home
and housing careers in the light of circumstances of the family of
origin, and there are inequalities which are clearly associated with
poverty and wealth. While wealthier families can provide a safety net
for their young when things go badly – by providing a home and
money – there are also young people from poorer families, perhaps
with lone mothers or with unemployed fathers, who may not be able
to return home so easily if things go wrong. There is thus inequality of
access to jobs, to housing, and to family support.

INDEPENDENCE, EMANCIPATION AND CITIZENSHIP

Leaving home and setting up an independent household should con-
firm young people as citizens in their own right, but does it? How and
between whom is citizenship negotiated? We have taken the case of
leaving home and forming households to further our argument that
notions of dependence and independence are simplistic, by suggesting that movement from one state to another is complex and long-
drawn out, and that the process is stratified and subject to modification. Indeed, the process is at the heart of the relationship between
young people and their families, as well as located in young people's
relations with the public institutions of the labour market and the
welfare state. Movement from the private world of childhood dependence in the family to adult citizenship in the public world of labour
markets, housing markets and political and civil institutions, is thus
structured both by pressures emanating from the family and by pressures coming from the state. In the middle of these often conflicting
pressures, there are young people seeking their independence: apparently willing to accept the responsibilities of adult citizenship but
often unable to gain access to the jobs, homes and welfare benefits
associated with citizenship rights.

Some moves away from the parental home are likely to be successful, though success will depend to a large extent on income, as Chapter 6 will indicate. The significance of leaving home as a stage in the
attainment of adult status in the 1990s varies considerably by social
class and gender, in ways which remain largely unaltered in recent
decades. But there have been changes, as young people appear to have
sought greater freedom outside marriage, and to have sought to resist
the economic dependence on their families which education, employment, training and welfare policies have tended to enforce on
them. It is particularly among the middle class that independent
households are set up prior to marriage, and this represents a new
form of emancipation, in Harris's (1983) terms, and indeed invests

more significance in the process of leaving home itself. But there have also been developments at the other end of the social scale. The more the Government seeks to place the responsibility for unemployment on the individual, or in the case of under-25s, their family, and to raise the qualification requirements for citizenship, the more young people have to assert their independence even if this involves taking greater risks. In extreme cases this means risking unemployment and homelessness for the sake of a minimal form of independence.

There are also gender differences. Women are likely to marry and have children younger than men and are often therefore further along a housing career than men. This does not necessarily mean that gender inequalities are reversed in the housing market, however; on the contrary, it reflects 'successful' socialization into gender roles. It is worth commenting here that while unemployment may slow down the process of family formation for men, it speeds up the process for women (Jones, 1990a; Phoenix 1991). However, there are also within-gender differences, which may be increasing over time. The emergence of single or peer group independent housing means that fewer women are moving straight from one situation of economic dependence to another, but are able to live independently, if only for a brief period before marriage or cohabitation. This could suggest (following Lister, 1990) that new opportunities for full participation are opening up for some women.

From this brief overview of young people's economic and household formation transitions, there emerges a picture of conflict between the normative values held by their public and private worlds, between the state and their families, even between the different institutions of the state. Young people may face contradictory messages and conflicting pressures. Rights and responsibilities are imposed on them, as they have no collective power with which to fight for change. Theirs is a relatively passive (and individualized) role, in so far as they are powerless to seek citizenship rights from their own collective base (see Turner, 1990, for a discussion of active and passive forms of citizenship). In their families, they can negotiate for emancipation rights, but they have little hope of claiming emancipation and the rights of citizenship in the public sphere.

Citizenship is not unitary and rights with respect to civil, political and social citizenship are not all conferred simultaneously; however, their access may later be structured by the individual's economic, marital, or household status. Perhaps as a result of this, or perhaps because there is an inherent conflict between the different aspects of citizenship, it appears that access to one set of rights may be structured by the presence of other rights, and we have seen how access to civil rights in the form of housing is determined by the right to social citizenship in the form of an income from social security – and indeed how political rights might be affected by both of these.

Young people are not a homogeneous grouping either. It is clear that the old structures of inequality – here we have mainly considered those resulting from capitalism and patriarchy – still operate to structure young people's lives, and that new patterns of transition are the consequence of constraint for some and opportunity and choice for others. If full participation in society were measured by marriage and parenthood, then women would have a great advantage over men, as they marry earlier. They are also apparently ahead of men in their housing careers. However, it is important to recognize here the distinction between rights and access. Women are likely to lose any newly-gained economic independence when they marry, so emancipation is unlikely to occur through marriage, and access to full participation in society likely to be limited (Lister, 1990). For women, then, the emergence of the apparently new phenomenon of single independent household may provide a key to citizenship between states of dependency, though access to independent households is structured and unequal. Social-class differences are equally important in structuring access. When the state takes away the safety net of social citizenship, some (wealthier) families can step in and provide financial assistance, food and housing, while others cannot. The divide is basically on social-class lines: it means that young people from poorer working-class families are more likely to need to assert, and find restricted access to, their social citizenship rights, and erosion of these rights means erosion of other rights of citizenship as well.

There is another dimension of inequality, the importance of which is becoming increasingly apparent: the rural/urban division (Midwinter and Monaghan, 1990). We suggested earlier that access to social citizenship rights has perhaps never been fully extended to people living in rural areas. It seems that young people in rural areas leave home and marry earlier than those in urban areas (see Wall, 1978, on the nineteenth century, and Jones, 1990a). For some women in rural areas, independence at least from the family of origin may be preferable to no independence at all; for other young people, access to citizenship may involve migration to towns.

6

CONSUMER

CITIZENS?

Youth has been extended by the formal structures of the education, labour market and welfare systems, but as we have indicated, there appears to be some assertion by young people of their rights to independent living. Hence, despite the risks, young people leave home even when there is no official support for them to do so. There is also a further anomaly, which is possibly not unrelated. Even though many are forced into extended economic dependency and excluded from the benefit system and the labour market, young people are nevertheless drawn into the consumer market at earlier ages. This is partly because the extension of dependency in youth encourages the creation of cultural groups, in some cases because young people may be freed from the burden of having to pay their way and, in other cases, because cultures develop out of resistance. One way or the other, 'student cultures' and 'trainee cultures' may be introduced. Partly, though, the young are drawn into consumption because this is in the interests of the market. Young people are important to consumer markets both because they spend on consumer artifacts now, and because in the near future, as householders and perhaps as parents they will form one of the major consumer groups. Their relationship with the market during youth will shape their future patterns of consumption.

During youth, access to consumer markets brings for some the possibility of new forms of freedom, independence and choice. This has implications for the 'individualization' of young people and for the construction of a self (Beck, 1986; Giddens, 1991). However, conversely, young people's choices in the market place, their power as consumers, are structured by their financial means. Their power is reduced when their income falls. Some are faced with real poverty.

Much of the consumption of young people is not related to their leisure or cultural styles at all, but concerns their day-to-day living expenses: for food, clothing and shelter. These needs change as young people leave their parents' homes and form new households and new families of their own. In order to examine the position of young people in the consumer market, we therefore have to take account, as in all other aspects of their lives, of the changes that are taking place as young people become adult, and of the inequalities which persist through youth or develop during it.

We will consider here the changing needs of young people, and the changing reaction of consumer markets to them. We consider the relationship between young people and the market in terms of inclusion and exclusion, as the most obvious form of inequality in this sphere. First, though, we review the research that has been done on leisure, culture and consumption to see how far young people's position has changed. We shall find that most of the research on spending in youth has focused on leisure and cultural forms, and neglected the issue of basic living costs. It has created an image of 'the young consumer', which has fuelled the enthusiasm of banks and other financial institutions to bring young people under their control (as spenders or investors of the future). We will question this image of the young consumer, and will consider whether the recent political emphasis on consumer citizenship has any relevance for young people in Britain today.

THEORIES OF YOUTH AND CONSUMPTION

In the sociology of youth, consumption and spending have been almost entirely identified in terms of the youth cultures and subcultures (which started in the late 1950s, a time of relative prosperity). For Parsons, youth cultures represented a means of transition from the home and into autonomous adulthood, helping the young person move from particularistic to universal roles (Parsons, 1973). Subsequent studies seem to have lost sight of the relevance of youth cultures as part of the *process* of youth, and have focused instead upon their more political significance as a form of resistance in youth. These subcultural studies highlighted the way in which youth subcultures were class-based and enabled young people to resolve or resist their various class positions (Hall and Jefferson, 1976; Mungham and Pearson, 1976; Brake, 1980). They concentrated upon working-class young men, because it was argued in the 1960s and 1970s that this was the group within which subcultures were most likely to develop. Student cultures of the same period tended to take a different form, and were more overtly political, but styles were still developed along class lines, in this case mainly middle class (Brake, 1980; Aggleton, 1987). Sociologists have continued to distinguish between 'rough' and 'respectable' cultural groups and Roberts (1983) argues that these divisions may have an increased salience in the context of rising unemployment. Membership of cultural groups is likely to be affected by the extension of dependence in youth, and the emergence or broadening of trainee and student groups, as we observed in Chapter 2. We would argue that while youth subcultures are important *per se*, they also have significance within the life course, since membership of groups changes as young people become adult, and consumption behaviour becomes dominated by needs rather than cultural styles.

The analysis of consumption encompasses the study of leisure more generally. The sociology of leisure is posited on a distinction between 'work' and 'leisure', in which each defines the other. The concept of leisure emerged from a traditional concept of stable employment based upon masculine experience in the labour market. The distinction between work time and non-work time has never been sustainable for those whose work is not restricted to structured positions in employment. Thus leisure has always been difficult to define in the case of women with domestic labour as well as or instead of paid work (see Deem, 1986) or for others whose work may include informal labour imposing other time constraints (Pahl, 1984). For those who are unemployed, the distinction between work time and leisure time has no meaning and time is constructed according to a non-work rhythm (Wallace, 1987a). For students and trainees too, work time may be flexible. Although the training schemes were designed to mimic the time-disciplines of employment, in practice neither tutors nor trainees on many of the schemes adhere rigidly to time discipline (Parsons, 1991). They are freer to define their own leisure time.

Leisure for all groups has become increasingly commercialized through the post-war period, and has become part of an enormous industry. Different leisure activities and life-styles are packaged and sold to particular targeted groups and few can now escape from capitalist relations and the market (Clarke and Critcher, 1985). Even private moments in private places such as the home are subject to this pervasive penetration, since the most consistently popular form of leisure activity for all age groups is watching television. Hence, in a late capitalist consumer economy, leisure increasingly means access to consumer markets. Through television, radio, magazines and communications media associated with the consumer markets, styles are promoted to young people. Consumer styles and artifacts come to be perceived as an integral part of their identity. Participation in these markets thus becomes a 'need', so that young people feel they need to be conspicuously sporting the latest styles and show their awareness of the latest trends, in order to be accepted in their peer groups. Within the sociology of youth, attention was first drawn to young people's roles as consumers in an influential paper by Abrams (1961), which argued that young people from working-class families coming into the labour market at 15 years had more disposable income than many other groups and could therefore generate a consumer market. This appears to have targeted them for exploitation.

Many have been critical of the effects of consumer markets on young people. The transition from a capitalist economy based on production to one based on consumption in many Western countries has resulted in the creation of a monolithic commercial culture. This is a form of oppression, according to the Frankfurt school of sociology. Cultural oppression and exploitation under capitalism operate as a form of social and political control and have encouraged greed, the pursuit of gratification and the ceaseless indulgence of the pleasure principle (see Marcuse, 1968). In these terms, consumer markets are likely to manipulate buyers and shape their patterns of consumption. Back in the 1950s and early 1960s, there was criticism of mass culture, seen by some to be degrading and corrupting young people, tempting them away from the classics of literature and into a shoddy imitation of American styles. Richard Hoggart (1958) for example, described the 'brief flowering' of the young working class after leaving school and before they were dragged down by the weight of parental responsibilities and hard lives of labour. During this period, young people were being manipulated by commercial consumerism, promoted by the mass media, and were betraying their working-class culture in favour of shallow, imported values.

Young people are targeted in particular ways as consumers of public and private services but also of consumer markets. The creation of a popular music industry, commercial dance halls and fashions all helped to shape a distinctive 'youth subculture'. However, according to Frith (1978), young people should not be characterized as passive leisure consumers. Instead, he suggests, young people actively participate in commercial consumption, selecting and differentiating between the different kinds of music on offer. Thus, they can shape the music market, and do have some power as consumers, though the effect is interactive. Music is one way in which subcultural groups define themselves – by following different genres and groups – and in which individuals can develop their own styles and tastes. The more recent theories, as we shall see, see access to consumer markets as representing a form of freedom and independence rather than oppression.

Consumer cultures

Since the 1980s, new ways of looking at culture and consumption have been developed. Influential amongst these have been ideas derived from 'post-modernism'. According to these arguments, most people in Britain share a common consumer culture through ready access to the mass media. The extensive production – or indeed 'over-production' – of images, signs and styles encourages a re-assembling of common identities around different themes: we are exhorted to develop individual tastes and unique styles based upon the assemblage of new images (Lash, 1990). We all inhabit a 'depthless consumer culture' in which signs and symbols can be re-interpreted. There is no need to go anywhere to achieve this – it is all accessible on television and radio at home. Indeed, we are more in touch with the world of multi-faceted consumer choice in our homes than on the streets. Thus, according to Lash (1990), mass consumer culture has an homogenizing influence as cultural consumption becomes generalized and is a differentiating factor as distinctive identities are developed within it: we may all watch *EastEnders* or the *Six O'Clock News* at some point but we still have our individual taste in programmes; we may all shop at Tesco's but we are encouraged to develop individual recipes and styles of eating. Cultural artifacts can be transformed and re-utilized in a different context – hence, Reebok trainers are important for defining status in a variety of contexts, only one of which is sport (for which they were presumably intended). In this context, individual 'taste' rather than structural location is important in determining consumption patters (Warde, 1990). Post-modernism tends to emphasize style and the analysis of images presented in consumer media, and neglects the role of structural inequalities. Thus subcultural class resistance and inequalities of access to consumption are not part of this analysis (see Hebdige, 1979; Martin, 1983).

The influence of post-modernism on sociological analysis has moved attention away from looking at participation based on class. As the production (or over-production) of consumer artifacts proliferates, so they come less and less to signify social classes or particular use-values, but become ends in themselves (Featherstone, 1990; Warde, 1990). Analyses of mass culture in a 'post-modern' age have stressed the way in which young people of all social classes and backgrounds have access to the same consumer images and artifacts and are able to re-group and manipulate these in order to create a variety of social identities independent of work status (Martin, 1983; Lash, 1990); thus, even those not in employment can construct a consumer identity.

Ulrich Beck (1986) has emphasized the way in which consumer markets and the labour market have created individual consumer choices and styles. The 'self' is constructed by the individual being forced to choose a personal style and to thread a way through increasingly individualized consumer and labour markets. Hartmann (1987) on the other hand has argued that individualization can be seen in the family setting, where young people are increasingly differentiated, having their own rooms, television sets, stereos and so on, and their own leisure lives over which their parents have decreasing control.

Whilst these ideas are helpful in directing us towards new ways of conceptualizing youth, they tend to assume a general level of affluence which in Britain we cannot take for granted.

Consumer citizenship

A further set of ideas, emanating from the 'New Right', defines consumer citizenship. Government policies since 1979 have been concerned with privatizing state assets and public utilities with the intention of creating free-market competition and consumer choice. A model of consumer choice has been introduced into public services as though they were services on the private market. For example, public transport passengers are described as 'customers' and areas of public transport privatized to give consumers a choice of services. The Citizen's Charter introduced by John Major in 1991 extends this idea to include consumer rights (including the right to complain about the new privatized services!). In the social and health services the idea of contract-compliance has been introduced, along with internal markets, and social service professionals have become on occasion the mediators between different service 'providers'. Under this system institutions which were previously centralized become customers of each other by contracting out. The individual consumer is the customer of the overall service. The privatization of housing through the emphasis on private purchase has the same consequence. In these conditions the idea of the Citizen's Charter enabling consumers to claim compensation for unsatisfactory services is wholly logical. In a society comprised of active consumers, citizenship is conferred by the relationship to both public and private consumer markets, and participation in consumer markets is an important aspect of citizenship as a whole.

This approach ignores, however, both the fact that participation in consumption depends upon income, and the way in which a consumer market encourages the emergence of different groups with differential access. Furthermore, it confuses consumption for cultural choice with consumption which is associated with basic needs. Choosing housing – a basic necessity of life – is on a different level to choosing television channels or a brand of shoes. The over-production of commodities in some markets, such as fashion industries, is matched by an under-production and shortage in others, such as housing. This idea of consumer citizenship both adds to and devalues Marshall's concept. For the 'New Right', citizenship no longer means the right to food, shelter and employment, rather it means the right to 'choose' between services. Choice is restricted to those with money.

Stratification in the consumer market

Consumption is stratified by social class, though other dimensions of inequality are increasingly being recognized. The expanding consumer market produces new evidence of differentiation, and continues the ongoing structural processes of stratification. Although class cultures may not be as distinctive as they were in the past, they still influence consumer styles in youth (Furlong, 1990).

The emphasis on youth cultures as reproduction of class cultures was challenged, first by feminists (McRobbie and Garber, 1976; MacDonald, 1980) and later by others pointing out the neglect of other sources of disadvantage including race and ethnicity, (dis)ability and sexual orientation (for example, Cross, 1987; Cross and Smith, 1987; Solomos, 1988). Social class is therefore not the only stratifying factor in the consumer market.

Feminists have drawn attention to the influence of gender in structuring consumer markets, and the role of markets in constructing gender. For working-class males obtaining a wage may be an important symbol of adult status because it gave access to various other consumer items – it afforded access to symbols of male adulthood through consumption – cigarettes, beer, motorbikes or cars. Indeed, in debates about the consequences of unemployment for young people there has been some discussion as to whether it is indeed a job which they miss the most or the money that comes from a job (Wallace, 1987a). Since the wages of young women are lower, they do not offer such a wide access to consumer markets (Hutton, 1991). They nevertheless provide access to adult femininity in the form of clothes, cosmetics and participation in places of entertainment. In magazines aimed at young women there is promotion of a narcissistic fascination with the self and the presentation of the self with the help of various commodities – hair shampoo, cosmetics and so on (McRobbie, 1991). Young women are encouraged to develop distinctive personal styles even on low incomes.

Women's consumer behaviour is however a more ambivalent signifier of power in the market. The adult female consumer purchases on behalf of others in the family rather than for herself, and the freedom of access to an income to spend is circumscribed by family roles (Deem, 1986; Pahl, 1991). However, McRobbie (1991) argues that young women can acquire a certain degree of independence and autonomy by participation in consumer markets even whilst living in their parental homes. She finds that young women's magazines are more likely to portray young women as in control of their lives and able to assert their own needs than they did in the past.

Consumer markets construct and perpetuate gender differences. Analysis of reading habits indicate very different patterns for males and females. The most popular magazines for young women, according to the National Readership Survey of 1987 tend to be about fashion, television, romance and the family, while young men are more likely to buy a range of soft-pornography or motoring magazines. It is clear from this that consumer interests are highly gender-specific. In the late 1980s a new genre of men's magazines arrived – those emphasizing style and fashion consumption for men; these magazines, such as Q, promoted more narcissistic pleasures for men more along the lines of the women's magazines, and made fatherhood into a fashion style. The media presentation of the 'new man' accessorized by a baby hardly relates to a reality of family life. Gender constructions are still reinforced by the consumer markets.

Young women are excluded in different ways from consumer participation, since their activities are controlled by sexual labelling and sexual danger so that home-centred activities are more common. The need to help with housework may be a factor in this (Griffin, 1985). Sue Lees (1986) has indicated the power of sexual labelling in limiting or circumscribing the participation of young people in youth cultures. Angela McRobbie (1991) too describes the situation of a group of young women in Birmingham who are excluded from the local youth cultures by early family responsibility, sexism of the men, and the fact that boyfriends controlled the income of the household, spending it all upon themselves. Young women had to fall back upon their own mothers for financial support even after they had left home and this was also the case in some examples from Wallace's study (1987a) of the Isle of Sheppey. However, this presents a rather grim picture of oppressed and depressed young working-class women, whereas an alternative picture could also be presented of young working-class women engaging with their environment and carving out an acceptable and independent role for themselves. Gender therefore operates to include and exclude men and women from consumer markets in particular ways.

The strength of this gender effect may vary in different youth groups, however. Studies within the 16–19 Initiative (Bynner, 1990) have indicated that gender divisions are dissolving or becoming more ambiguous. This is the case particularly among students, who tend to be a more homogeneous group in gender terms. In one study it emerged that there were common youth leisure pursuits, including going to pubs and discos and listening to records, although young women were still more inclined towards reading and going to cinemas, theatres and concerts, and more males were drinking, betting and watching sport (Roberts *et al.*, 1991). The more established view of girls' leisure is that it takes place as part of a 'bedroom culture' rather than on the streets and that it is more passive and commercially manipulated than male pursuits (McRobbie and Garber, 1976). Changes over the last decade now suggest that this rather 'over-socialized' view of girls has become less appropriate, since young women are often now taking a more obvious part in subcultural activities. Deem (1986) has stressed that there are gender differences among adults in access to leisure, since women with family responsibilities have little time to themselves. However, for those young people who are not yet embarked on domestic trajectories there is an increasing convergence between male and female leisure activities in all social classes.

Race and ethnicity influence 'niche marketing' and patterns of consumption which are related to the different position of ethnic groups in the labour market. Again though the relationship is two-way, and ethnic minority groups have had their own influence upon consumer markets and popular styles for young people (see Hebdige, 1979; and Hewitt, 1988 for studies of the influence of black youth culture upon white ones). Nevertheless, the disadvantages suffered by members of some ethnic minorities in terms of their likelihood of unemployment or low-paid jobs, limit their access to consumer markets. Their access is further limited by the fact that consumer markets on the whole reflect a dominant white hegemony which serves to exclude and marginalize ethnic minority groups.

Finally, disabled young people suffer particular disadvantages in terms of increased dependency upon parents and low-paid jobs and these mean that they have less independent consumer power than other groups. Places of entertainment and shops tend to cater for (and assume) able-bodied customers, thus marginalizing the experience of those who are disabled.

Although the emerging sociology of consumption has sought to emphasize the liberating potential of consumer markets and consumer choice and the possibilities these have for individual styles, access to consumer markets is still stratified. The material differences in young people's access are underplayed or ignored. Whilst in some respects new associations become possible, in other respects old inequalities persist.

New forms of stratification

With the rise of youth unemployment and extension of education and training, new social divisions have developed. Furthermore, the drop in income of young people and the stark and conspicuous poverty of some groups in the 1980s have highlighted the fact that studies of affluent consumers and subcultures had failed to take into account the needs and costs of young people growing up. Expenditure should be seen in terms of the consumption of basic needs, including housing expenditure, as well as spending on fashion and popular music. If young people are no longer affluent consumers then what is their role in consumer markets? In the context of the 1990s this depends crucially upon the role of the family and parental support for young people.

New patterns of transition into the labour market have structured inequality in the consumer markets. For example, analysis of the Scottish Young People's Survey and the 16–19 Initiative studies have indicated that young people's access to consumption is affected by their economic status, and increased likelihood of being in intermediate institutions between school and the labour market (Roberts *et al.*, 1991). The unemployed and YTS trainees (with incomes of around £30 a week) had the most restricted access to consumption and leisure, while the employed, with average incomes of around £80, had far more access to leisure. However, the group to emerge as most 'leisure rich' were the students, although their incomes were only about £40 a week (Roberts *et al.*, 1991: 133):

> In almost every respect the students were the most leisure-privileged, whilst the unemployed were the most deprived. The students had the highest overall level of recreational activity due to their greater involvement in playing sport, reading, going to cinemas, theatres, concerts, exhibitions, galleries, museums and churches and for meals out. There were only two kinds of leisure where respondents in jobs were the most active – watching sport and betting ...

These authors also found students had the widest social networks. They conclude that studenthood adds to the cumulative benefits of those on the 'academic' career track who get better jobs eventually and have greater access to consumer markets in the meantime. One argument against this interpretation is that many of these activities, in the case of students, are on the borderline between work and leisure. Students, it seems, can draw on subsidized leisure, are more likely to be able to get financial help from their families, and can also, in Bourdieu's terminology, draw on cultural capital (Bourdieu and Passeron, 1977) to enhance their consumer power. However, this does not detract from the main finding, that economic status structures access to leisure consumption (just as economic status fundamentally structures leisure time, as we have indicated). Work in the labour market imposes structural constraints on leisure time but also provides an income and thence access to leisure consumption. Unemployment provides unstructured time, but no access. Traineeship and studenthood produce intermediate positions in both respects.

PARTICIPATION IN CONSUMER MARKETS

It is important to look beyond leisure, though. Young people also spend on their basic needs, and it is important to understand both what these needs are and how young people should be expected to pay for them. Access to consumer markets depends upon access to an income. During the 1980s social strata were re-composed such that an increasing gulf emerged, the 'wealth divide', between those who benefited from the prosperity of the Thatcher years and were able to participate in the consumer boom and those who were increasingly excluded. Young people are on the whole in the bottom half of this wealth divide. They, along with the elderly and lone mothers, form the poorest social groups in Britain.

Credit and banking

Although young people's income from wages and from social security and grants has dropped, other opportunities for income have opened up. In some cases, parents help to equalize the income of children out of work (see Hutson and Jenkins, 1989), or use credit to subsidize the incomes of their children. Another possibility is that young people make more use of their own extended access to credit.

Credit and banking facilities have been opened to younger and younger children and this was facilitated by the de-regulation of credit in the 1980s. A survey by the Halifax Building Society carried out amongst 5000 of its young customers in 1989 found that even children under the age of 12 had long-term savings and were saving for houses, cars and holidays. In a survey of the South-West of England by Wallace and colleagues (1991b), 18- and 19-year-olds were saving a median sum of £10 per week and were left with a median sum of £15 per week to spend on what they wanted. Savings are, however, only one side of this coin. About 10 per cent of the sample had taken out a loan or overdraft in the last year and the median sum of the loan was £1000. The main reason for taking out such a loan, in 63 per cent of cases, was to buy a car; 16 per cent of those with loans were students.

Qualitative interviews revealed that young people on low incomes often had substantial debts to credit companies, banks and catalogue companies (Wallace, 1991c). This then is the down side of the credit boom.

Hutton (1991), in a quasi-cohort analysis of the Family Expenditure Survey, found that the use of credit had risen among young people in recent decades. Thus involvement in financial institutions facilitated participation in consumer markets. However, it also attached young people individually to debt in financial institutions. Other sources have indicated that young people are increasingly hooked into financial institutions by the time they reach their twenties. The National Opinion Poll data shown in Figure 6.1 indicates that young people had a variety of investments, particularly in banks and building societies, and that store accounts, loans and credit cards were fairly common. The poll found that young men were marginally more likely to have access to these things than young women, although the main differentiating feature was age. This reflected age differences in earned and disposable incomes.

In the past, the working-class youth wage provided access to consumer markets. This allowed working-class young people the 'brief

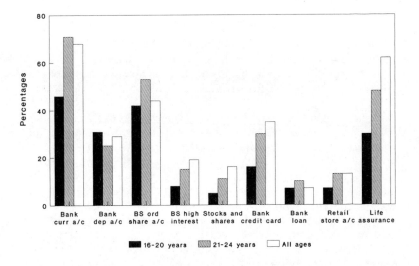

Figure 6.1   Banking and credit cards by age
Source: National Opinion Poll *Financial Research Survey*, April–September 1987

flowering' (Hoggart, 1958) of consumer freedom in their teens during which time they were defined as 'affluent consumers' (Abrams, 1961), and their spending and leisure styles set the street trends in the 'swinging sixties'. Students, on the other hand, were expected to defer their gratification until they had finished studying and found jobs; they could then join the burgeoning consumer markets. The connection in both cases between employment and consumption has been broken by the insertion of intermediate states, characterized by low incomes. It has also been broken because consumer markets have opened up to embrace younger customers who are still in education. This has created a scissors effect: consumption has become an important part of youth, while incomes have dwindled.

Participation in consumer markets can also have a positive side. Consumption can be a source of power, social status and identity even without occupational status. It can lead to a certain degree of self-determination and acceptance as a consumer citizen within the community. Young people are therefore socialized into becoming consumer citizens – their 'needs' are shaped by consumer markets and parents are under pressure too to provide for these needs. It is important to distinguish between different groups of young people and take into account the increasing polarization between those with secure economic and family support and those who lack those things. The 1980s was the decade of the cardboard cities as well as of the 'yuppie'.

Spending on essential needs

During the years of young adulthood, most people move into independent housing. Though Roberts (1981) has suggested that leisure activity may be changing during this transition, it is important to understand how spending on essential needs, such as food, clothing and housing, may be changing at the same time. Piachaud (1982) has stressed the need to study shifting expenditure patterns, and in particular to study acquisition of consumer goods according to a life-course model, on the basis that acquisition of consumer durables, for example, is structured by age and domestic responsibility. Dale (1987) has shown how household ownership of consumer durables relates to stage in the family life cycle. The period of household formation in youth is likely to be a period when spending patterns begin to become more home-centred, shifting from expenditure on leisure activities to expenditure which is more directly related to the costs of independent living. We have seen in Chapter 4 how this process starts with the payment of board money while young people are living with their parents. The shift from leisure expenditure to domestic expenditure speeds up with the process of leaving home, as setting up a household is a costly business.

Table 6.1   The costs of setting up home for two

Household item	Budget (£)	
	Basic	Recommended
Furniture and consumer durables	706	3484
Soft furnishings and floor coverings	240	750
Bedding and linen	103	383
Kitchenware	74	473
Crockery, glass and cutlery	26	227
General household items	50	216
Total	1199	5533

Source: Walker, 1988 (table 2.8)

Table 6.1 shows the basic minimum and recommended costs estimated by Walker (1988) of setting up a home for two people. Walker argues that it is the 'recommended' set of figures which is the more realistic, yet few young people setting up independent households are likely to have resources of this magnitude. Kirk *et al.* (1991) estimated that a young person setting up home would need a lump sum of at least £1500 for essentials such as basic furniture, floor coverings and kitchen equipment, and a weekly income of £43 (1990 estimate) for basic maintenance (food, fuel, travel, household costs and personal expenditure). Young people are unlikely to be eligible for amounts such as these from social security sources, assuming they are eligible for social security at all. This means that many young people start their independent living situations with severe financial problems, unless they are in receipt of a good income, or receiving financial help from their families. A higher income is therefore likely to be a factor in the age of leaving home, according to Ermisch and Overton (1984).

Claire Wallace's study (1987a) of young people on the Isle of Sheppey has indicated that as young people become adult they become more instrumentally orientated, putting more money towards the home. Indeed for some, consumption patterns may be more significant than career goals at this stage, and success measured in terms of property rather than prospects. Unemployment may not radically alter this basic orientation: Hutson and Jenkins (1987) suggest that young people have been so socialized into 'commitment to the mainstream values of consumerist accumulation' that even the long-term unemployed are locked into the consumer durable market.

A fairly recent marketing survey (Marketing Directions Ltd, 1988) shows the level of ownership of consumer durables which are associated with leisure. Two-thirds of young people in the marketing survey had access to a colour television set, more than half had access to a video recorder, nearly one-third had access to a personal stereo and between one-quarter and one-third had access to a home computer. These consumer goods allow for connection with wider consumer markets and also for the construction of a separate identity even for those living in the parental home. Thus it is not only access to consumption which is important but also access to the means of consumption – the equipment and materials such as videos and cars – which enable full participation in cultural life.

Sandra Hutton's analysis (1991) of the Family Expenditure Survey has included a comparison of the income and spending patterns of cohorts of 16–25-year-olds in the 1960s, 1970s and 1980s. She found that the proportion of all young people with an income from earnings declined over the 1970s and 1980s: numbers of those receiving income support or supplementary benefits rose by 21 per cent and those receiving unemployment benefits by 10 per cent. Partly as a result, real incomes of those in the range 16–22 years had fallen. However, at the same time, expenditure on food, alcohol, transport and clothes had risen in this age group, though expenditure on clothing dropped again in the 1980s. The implication is that young people in the 1980s must have found other sources of income to finance this increase in their living costs. The most recent cohort also owned more consumer durables and were more likely to own their own house than the equivalent cohort 20 years ago.

Definitions of need and luxury vary, as Kirk *et al.* (1991) have pointed out. Their research on young people who had left home in Edinburgh found quite different perceptions of need in different groups of young people (students, trainees, unemployed, single parents). These researchers asked young people what they would call a real luxury: some suggested spending on entertainment and leisure, others suggested food, clothes, or 'something for the home'. A single parent said a baby-sitter would be a real luxury. A 'poverty of expectations' was identified in many of the responses – where expectations were severely constrained and hopes very limited.

Young people in the housing market

Housing requires one of the most essential forms of expenditure, and the cost of housing is gradually taken on in youth, starting with the payment of board money to parents (see Chapter 4) and extending when young people leave their homes of origin. We saw in Chapter 5 that most people have left their parental homes by the age of 22, some very much earlier, though not all enter the housing market when they leave (some go into hostel accommodation, live with relatives, or take up jobs with accommodation attached). Others, however, have to compete despite their limited resources in a dwindling market.

The housing market creates cleavages between different types of tenure groups, and these cleavages according to some are now as important as stratification by social class (Saunders, 1986). It is difficult to apply this model to young people, though, just as it is difficult to locate young people in a particular social class (see Jones, 1987a) because of the transitional processes involved. Young people may be on career mobility routes in the occupational class structure, but they are also involved in careers in the housing market. They are also in transitional economic statuses, students or trainees, as we have indicated.

Different groups of young people (students, workers, parents or couples with families) occupy different places within the housing market. The trend for some time has been towards encouraging owner occupation through tax subsidies and explicit government policies, so that over 60 per cent of all householders are now owner occupiers. Young people are largely excluded from this sector due to their low incomes and instability of employment, but during the 1970s, building societies were encouraged to extend mortgages to wider groups of people – manual workers, young people, single people and cohabiting couples – all categories who may have found it difficult to gain access to owner occupation previously. Hence, 35 per cent of householders under the age of 24 were owner occupiers in 1986 and this had risen from 31 per cent in 1971 (*Social Trends 19*, 1989). This is particularly high in comparison with patterns in other western industrial countries (indicating that young people in Britain have more financial responsibilities). Walker (1988) reports the discrepancy between preference and practice in this respect: in 1982, while 84 per cent of people aged 20–24 expressed a preference for owner occupation, only 30 per cent were in fact owners. He points out that in the case of low-paid workers, home ownership is only a realistic proposition if they happen to live in a low-cost area, or if partners can contribute a substantial income, and thus younger married couples are more likely to rent, or share with in-laws.

Public-sector housing is intended to provide for those excluded from private housing but young people are to a great extent excluded from this sector too. Tenancies are not legally available in England and Wales under the age of 18. Local authorities have pursued fairly conservative ideas of re-housing based upon 'points' systems in which being a parent with children will score more highly. Housing associations which are expanding to fill the space left by the decline of local authority housing are likely to pursue similar policies in many areas: strong priority is placed upon housing families with dependent children. The public-housing sector has declined during the 1980s on account of the 'right to buy' policies on the one hand and because financial constraints have prevented local authorities from building new housing on the other. Public housing is becoming increasingly 'residualized' as a result, but it nevertheless still accounts for 26 per cent of all tenures. Thirty per cent of those under the age of 24 were in local authority tenancies, but this had risen from 21 per cent in 1971 (*Social Trends 19*, 1989). This may reflect the fact that some local authorities have made their 'hard to let' high rise and other accommodation to young people. According to Murphy and Sullivan (1986) there is a 'filtering' effect amongst young householders, whereby those who are unemployed increasingly find that local authority housing is their only possibility and they are joined by those who become unemployed, cannot maintain mortgage payments, and have their homes re-possessed.

The privately-rented sector is the main source of accommodation to young people leaving their parents' home. Although a minority tenure across all age groups, accounting for just 11 per cent overall, 35 per cent of householders under 24 lived in such accommodation, but this had declined from 57 per cent in 1971 (*Social Trends* 19,1989). Tenants in this sector enjoyed some protection in legislation after the Second World War, but much of this was swept away in the 1980s with de-regulation of rents and tenancies from 1988. This was intended to boost the market but it also made the position of tenants more insecure and their rents higher. Board and lodgings regulations (see Chapter 3) affect patterns of entry into the private rented sectors in particular; the legislation assumes that young people can return to a nurturing parental home, yet there is growing evidence that this is not always the case (Mathews, 1986; Jones, 1991a). Moreover, the privately rented sector is notorious for high rents, poor quality property (often multi-occupied) and insecurity of tenure.

These different tenures may represent different stages in a housing career, as Gill Jones (1987b) has indicated. Her analysis of the NCDS and GHS suggests that young people may move from their parental homes into 'transitional' housing before finding more permanent accommodation in the public-rented sector or buying their own first homes. This 'transitional' housing, while insecure and sometimes fraught with problems, nevertheless may allow flexibility in the housing market which may be needed when young people are first entering employment and, on occasion, needing to be geographically mobile in order to find work.

The housing situation of young people is also related to their economic status. Young people enter the housing market with different needs, at different ages, and with different sources of income. Students have tended to occupy a distinct housing sector of privately-rented, temporary accommodation and most major cities with

polytechnics and universities have a 'student quarter' catering specifically to their needs. This may consist of student halls of residence,
lodgings in private homes or furnished accommodation in bedsits or
flats and shared houses. This high-density communal accommodation has hitherto been subsidized by student grants and local authority housing benefit, although as the housing benefit was withdrawn
in 1990, patterns may now change as students will not be able to
maintain their dominance of the private rented sector. Although students generally have to leave home in order to attend a course, trainees are not expected to leave home and there is no housing element in
their training allowance for them to do so.

Young people's location in the housing market was always pre-
carious, but in the 1980s it became further squeezed for a variety of
reasons. The redevelopment of inner city centres had displaced young
people from the low-cost rented sector which they had traditionally
occupied. The more long-term decline in privately-rented accommodation and the effects of de-regulation of rents meant that such housing has disappeared or become much more expensive – beyond the
reach of young people. The fiscal squeeze in the 1970s and 1980s
meant that subsidies of various kinds to young householders had
declined (see Chapter 3) and this was manifested in the decline in rent
subsidies and the decline in local authority or housing association
building. The housing that was built, tended to be designed for families (Burton *et al.* 1989).

Homelessness

The contraction of the housing market catering for young people
coincided with the reduction in their incomes, so that the housing
that was available was not affordable, and they could no longer compete in the market. There have been various outcomes. Young people
appear increasingly to have been returning to their parents' homes,
because of the shortages of jobs and housing; those in the housing
market have increasingly taken on accommodation which they could
not afford; others have dropped out of the housing market altogether
and become homeless.

Homelessness is now affecting more and more young people. The
response of the Government has been to encourage young people to
return home to their families, rather than to improve their chances in
the housing market by providing affordable and appropriate accommodation, and incomes. This, like the policies affecting training and
employment, serves once again to re-define youth and extend the
period of dependence of young people on their families (mainly with
a view to decreasing the dependence of some on the state).

Many of the housing needs of young people are concealed by the fact that they are inadequately housed on other people's floors, or in parental accommodation where they no longer wish to live, in circumstances of 'hidden homelessness' (Roof, 1982). Some argue that their situation is exacerbated by family tension following unemployment, the exit from board and lodgings under the new regulations and the inability of young people to compete with wealthier adults for rented accommodation (Cusack and Roll 1985). Young people leaving long-term care may have an additional problem once they cease to be the responsibility of local authorities at the age of 18 or earlier (Stein and Carey, 1986), and indeed one-third of all single homeless appear to have been in care (Department of Environment, 1981).

In London, and indeed other large cities in Britain, the colonies of young people living in cardboard boxes or begging on the streets attest to the fact that although there may be more jobs there, there are fewer places to live (Randall, 1988; O'Mahoney, 1988). Many young people migrate to London; as many as 1700 homeless young people a year go through Centrepoint hostel alone and there are an estimated 50 000 more in temporary shelters. Some 2000 are thought to live in squats and 45 000 in other inappropriate circumstances, such as sleeping on friends' floors. These latter would not even be counted in the official homelessness figures (Randall, 1988).

The problem is not limited to urban areas. There may be limited availability of public-sector rented accommodation in rural areas, and the private-sector costs are driven up by wealthier city-dwellers who rent or buy second homes. The privately-rented sector is dominated by seasonal holiday accommodation. Some holiday accommodation can be converted to housing the homeless and instead of 'cardboard cities' there are 'caravan and chalet villages' which are intended for temporary occupation but in fact provide housing all year round for those with nothing else (Wallace, 1991c). Since the shortage of housing is paralleled by the shortage of jobs and courses in rural areas, many young people have no choice but to migrate to the towns (Jones, 1990a), though it is by no means certain that they will find either, once they get there.

A study carried out in Wales by Hutson and Liddiard (1991) found at least 2000 young people without homes. They found that there were fewer young women in this situation and speculate that they may be more able to form sexual relationships with male partners which will provide them with accommodation (though an alternative explanation is that women are more likely to be housed by local authority housing departments, and are less likely to be longer-term homeless for this reason). In Wales the young homeless would stay in their own area for a while and then migrate to Cardiff where there were more agencies for dealing with them. A large number of the homeless young people mentioned family problems as a reason for not returning home (Hutson and Liddiard, 1991).

The problems of housing for young people are compounded by other problems. The problems for 16–18-year-olds are particularly acute as they are not necessarily entitled to any income maintenance, and in England and Wales are not legally entitled to sign a tenancy agreement. Hence a study in South-West England found a young man and his pregnant girlfriend living in a caravan on £15 per fortnight plus housing benefit (Wallace, 1991c). They were unable to turn to their parents because one set of parents was facing bankruptcy and the others had withdrawn support for the couple. They were sinking into debt in order to keep going, to the extent that even if they had found work, they would have little left to spend after paying off the debts.

YOUTH POVERTY

Most of the studies of consumption and living costs in youth have not been able to assess the extent and nature of familial support for young people although this would appear to be crucial. Where parents cannot or will not support their children the result can be considerable hardship and poverty.

Since the re-discovery of poverty in Britain in the 1960s, the debate has stressed the importance of relative rather than absolute poverty: relative poverty echoes Marshall's original concept of the rights of social citizenship as the right to live the life of a 'civilized being according to the standards prevailing in the society' (Marshall, 1949). Hence Townsend (1979) argued that if people could afford holidays or television sets they could be in relative poverty if these are part of 'normal' living conditions in Britain today. Absolute poverty was where a person lacked even the basic subsistence for survival: food, shelter and clothing. Even Townsend and colleagues did not think this kind of poverty persisted very widely in affluent post-war Britain. The Conservatives in the 1980s, on the other hand, using the yardstick of absolute poverty, argued that poverty did not exist at all.

Occasional reports have revealed absolute poverty among young people in Britain, through cases where young people were homeless or had insufficient to eat (Kirk *et al.*, 1991). In 1980s' Britain, an unprecedented consumer boom was paralleled by large numbers of young people becoming pauperized. Young people have been a particularly vulnerable group in this respect because of changes in social security and the labour market. Together with lone mothers and the elderly, young people are among the poorest members of society. As Lister (1991) has pointed out, this affects citizenship status: in our example of young people, if they can no longer participate in consumer society and are not seen as having a right to resources such as housing, leisure and food, they become second- or even third-class citizens (as Kirk *et al.*, 1991, have indicated).

Young people who are homeless and penniless are, in addition, at risk of exploitation and getting into criminal activity, often in order to survive (Kirk *et al.*, 1991; MORI, 1991). Peelo *et al.* (1990) in a study of young offenders in England identified a life-style of disruption and brutality experienced at home accompanied by homelessness, drifting from place to place and surviving on crime or immoral earnings. They describe the case of Carol who was aged 17, on a training scheme and officially living with her parents; she needed help with housing costs and furniture to set up home, but, as her probation officer pointed out, though Carol suffered physical and emotional abuse at home, she was reluctant and too embarrassed to try to prove her distress to the DSS. Kirk *et al.* (1991: 17) quote 17-year-old Marjory's experience at the DSS, after she too had suffered abuse at home:

> Well, I thought the woman was a nosy boot, actually, ken, because she wants ... she asks you about absolutely everything, ken, that's got nothing to do with it, ken what I mean? I don't know – I don't think people should have to sit through that just to get money. She was asking things like, 'And what made you leave home? So why can't you go back?' ken, things like that. It's got nothing to do with her.

These examples graphically illustrate the problems of young people who do not receive family support and are consequently unable under current conditions to secure a place for themselves in the labour and housing markets. Their prospects have declined in the 1980s and 1990s.

INCLUSION AND EXCLUSION

The concept of consumer citizenship stratifies between those who have and those who have not. There are thus contradictory tendencies: on the one hand, young people have reduced incomes and many suffer extreme poverty; on the other hand, consumer markets offer the prospect of power and independence to all young people. Access to the 'carrot' of consumer citizenship is limited. How can we conceptualize youth in this context?

Drawing upon the concepts presented by Kirk and colleagues (1991) we can identify increasing divergence between inclusion in cultural life and exclusion from the prevailing standard of living. People might share cultural symbols and language derived from mass media communications, but they do not share the means to buy consumer artifacts. Despite this restricted access to the consumer market, cultural symbols may nevertheless take on greater significance in circumstances where individual status is devalued – as a trainee or as an unemployed person, for example. The fractured nature of transitions in youth makes it more difficult to define status by employment, but it may also produce the 'freedom' to define and develop new cultural identities, sometimes in consumption terms. The division between spending as leisure and spending as need may thus on occasion become blurred, since spending on leisure may form for some a strategy of survival.

Apart from access to the time and money for leisure, access to transport can be important too. Marketing surveys indicate the importance of a driving licence or access to private transport in youth: 46 per cent of young people aged 18 held a driving licence and this had gone up to 58 per cent by the age of 20 (Marketing Directions Ltd, 1988). Furthermore, 26 per cent of young men and 17 per cent of young women were car-owners in 1988. Wallace found that car ownership was particularly a priority in rural areas (Wallace *et al.*, 1991a), as transport allowed access to both work and leisure, enabling fuller participation in cultural life.

What happens to those young people who are excluded from much consumer participation? Jeremy Seabrook (1982) paints a dismal picture of young people locked out of mainstream consumer culture if they are unemployed, wandering around the shopping malls stacked with glittering consumer prizes and unable to reach them. Mike Presdee (1990) describes a similar situation in Australia, where young unemployed are attracted to the big, security-patrolled shopping arcades ('cathedrals of capitalism') which are organized around expenditure and have no space for non-consumers. Excluded from consumer citizenship, the young men interviewed resorted to alternative forms of status: their world became a fight over the right to occupy space as a non-consumer in a consumer-oriented world (Presdee, 1990; White, 1990). Alternatively, they could resort to fantasized status and conspicuous consumption of any money they did come across by 'blowing it' (Wallace, 1987a) – though as Kirk *et al.* (1991) indicate, 'blowing it' could include anything from buying stereo equipment or a camera, to paying off debts.

CONSUMER CITIZENS?

In Chapter 2 we discussed the changing situation of young people in relation to the labour market. The transition from school to work has become more complex and extended, and intermediate statuses have emerged between the economic dependence associated with full-time education, and the economic independence associated with full-time employment. More young people are filling the intermediate statuses of college student or trainee, and routes have become more unclear and more individualized. Access to consumer markets gives some young people the ability to re-make their social identities around their consumer choices, for example in styles of music or dress. Their leisure patterns and 'life-styles' are thus being re-shaped around the new status-passages which have been constructed.

Whilst the emphasis on leisure and consumption points towards individualization, or stratification based upon consumer groups, this ignores the way in which spending is circumscribed by material factors. The universal consumer culture has set up a new form of stratified citizenship in which those who have no income (from work, their families or social security) are second-class, or even third-class citizens (Kirk *et al.*, 1991; Lister, 1991). On the other hand, consumer power (in so far as this extends to young consumers) allows some young people to have a degree of autonomy and individuation whilst remaining dependent upon their parents. We have seen how young people are inserted into formal financial relations of consumption and banking at an earlier age: this is in direct contrast to their increasingly extended dependency in other respects.

Access to the consumer markets may depend more and more on whether young people are able to get financial help from their families, and poverty is most likely to occur where this is not forthcoming, either because of estrangement from parents, or because parents are themselves having difficulty in making ends meet. While young people are living in their parental homes, their position may be, as Lydia Morris (1990) indicates, as 'partially-dependent consumers' within the household. They have some disposable income of their own, but this depends upon the quality of their relationship with their parents (or surrogate parents), and on the latter's own financial circumstances. The leisure activities of young people may have a particularly privileged position within the family and be supported by parents, when the continuation of close relations between parents and children may be based upon indulgent 'spoiling' by parents (Leonard, 1980). Given the high costs of living and the low incomes of young people generally, there is now an increased and more widespread need for parental support.

Paradoxically, at the same time as state support is withdrawn and young people are forced to become more dependent upon parents, the market process has served to construct them as independent consumer citizens firstly by offering more and more choice and secondly by locking them into financial markets and socializing them into becoming contemporary 'conspicuous spenders'. This is particularly unfortunate for those who are not able to negotiate sufficient funds from parents, or whose parents are themselves poor. We have seen various instances of the increase in indebtedness in youth, which is one outcome of this market process. The concept of consumer citizenship involves the right to choose between services, but, as we have indicated, essential needs have to be meet – the needs for food, clothing and shelter – before young people can have the luxury of real choice in the consumer market.

7

RE-THINKING YOUTH

AND CITIZENSHIP

It is important to understand how young people move through the process of youth to become independent participants in society. Equally, it is important to recognize the structural inequalities which create opportunities and constraints during youth and thus shape the process of youth itself. We have argued therefore for youth to be understood in terms of process and structure. For this approach to be successful, it is also important to re-integrate the concepts of the public and the private spheres – often separated in theory though they have so many points of interaction in practice. Only then can we evaluate the extent to which young people's lives as a whole are determined by constraints, and the extent to which they are able to exercise self-determination in creating their own biographies, bearing in mind that there is inequality in youth, and that there are degrees of constraint and choice. Bertaux (1981) argued that it is only by studying the differential experiences of different social groups during their life courses that we can bring biography into the realms of sociology. Only then can the complexity of young people's lives be understood and can sociology begin to offer constructive criticism of social policies affecting young people.

A life-course approach should allow study both of the processes which occur during youth, and of the way in which young people negotiate their personal biographies through formal and informal institutional structures which are themselves changing over time. As our review has shown, there remain many gaps in our knowledge of young people's perceptions of the structures which shape their lives, and their understanding of the process of becoming adult. If we are to understand youth as a part of the 'reflexive project' (Giddens, 1991) of a lifetime biography, then research is still needed to understand the 'strategies' young people use to negotiate their ways through the maze of public and private institutions structuring their youth.

Where processes in youth have been studied, these have tended to focus on paths through formal structures, such as education and the labour market, and there has been relative neglect of young people's transitions in the informal structures of family life. The private sphere of young people's family roles and relationships has remained shut off from social scientists and policy-makers alike, in a proverbial 'black box'. The myth of the traditional family, with parents caring for, and controlling, their children until they are ready to fly the nest, has been perpetuated, and we have seen the effects of this in social policies over many years. It is important to open up this black box, and to examine the family roles and relationships of young people *in the context* of their roles and relationships in more formal settings outside their families, thus removing the artificial separation of the public and the private spheres.

In the course of our exploration, we have been evaluating two different approaches to the study of young people's lives, that which stresses structure and determinism, and that which emphasizes agency and self-determination. The life-course approach allows us to see these two perspectives not as conflicting but as compatible. While the social structure of stratification, based largely on social class, gender, race and ethnic inequalities, affects young people's life chances from birth, during their life course they steer their way, with varying degrees of success, through formal and informal institutional structures, which put new constraints and opportunities in their paths; structural inequalities mean that there are more opportunities for some and more constraints for others, so that some young people's actions may clearly be seen as informed choice strategies, arising from opportunity, and others as survival strategies, arising from constraint. The approaches are not polarized, the extent to which agency or structure predominates is more a question of degree.

We have reviewed and identified the ways in which formal institutions of the state and the market-place have structured young people's lives as dependent or independent. We have considered how the circumstances of their families and the expectations of their parents may affect young people's biographies and their dependency status. We have considered how young people try to make the move to independence, as workers, householders and consumers, and the obstacles which may lie in their paths. We have also sought to integrate often separated aspects of young people's lives, within an overall framework of change over the life course in youth, and change over historical time in the structures and policies which constrain or open up opportunities for young people to determine their own biographies.

Our aim has been to broaden out the sociology of youth, so that it can inform social policies as well as criticize them. We have discussed some of the limitations apparent in the sociology of youth – limitations which are repeated, with a potentially far worse effect, in the policies of the state. The lack of understanding of the process of youth, the lack of awareness of heterogeneity and inequality in youth, and the lack of a holistic approach to youth have all been replicated in social policies directed at young people.

In consequence, young people are getting a very raw deal these days, and constraints are beginning to outweigh opportunities in many more cases. While more and more young people are able to take advantage of increased educational and training opportunities, there are also more and more young people who are suffering from unemployment, homelessness and poverty and who seem to be lacking basic human rights to food, clothing and shelter. These are at the end of a continuum of disadvantage, which appears to be extending up the social spectrum. It is thus not just the unemployed who are disadvantaged, but also those who are coping with low incomes on training schemes, and students, too, who are increasingly likely to be accruing unmanageable debts. Disadvantage in youth is stratified – people at the bottom end of the social spectrum suffer the greatest disadvantage – but young people as a whole are suffering increasing disadvantage too. Their problem is that as a heterogeneous grouping, bound only by their age and their location in historical time, they have no organized voice, and indeed cannot easily be represented. They have been left out of political lobbies such as the trade union movement, political parties, pressure groups (with the notable exception of Youthaid). It seems to us particularly ironic that in an era when all political parties are stressing individual rights, young people are so obviously excluded from the rhetoric. Their rights and responsibilities need acknowledgement too.

YOUTH AND CITIZENSHIP

The concept which best embodies a package of rights and responsibilities associated with full membership of (and representation in) society, is that of citizenship. Here we have applied the concept of citizenship to the study of youth in various ways: we have considered the modern concept in terms of its civil, political and social dimensions as formulated by Marshall (1950), but we have also extended this analysis. First, we have considered citizenship in terms of rights and responsibilities of young people, in both the public and the private spheres of their lives. Second, we have taken on board Ruth

Lister's approach to citizenship among women (Lister, 1990, 1991), in particular her argument that full citizenship is possible only where there is economic independence. Third, we have questioned the ideology that in nuclear families, dependants can acquire the rights of citizenship by proxy, through the head of household. Fourth, we have problematized the concept of dependence in youth. Finally, we have considered whether the most recent manifestation of citizenship in public debate, that of consumer citizenship, or power through choice in the consumer market, can be applied to young people.

Let us review some of the arguments, and consider the value of the citizenship thesis to theory and policy with regard to young people. Some current dilemmas faced by policy-makers are considered: between allowing responsibilities to rest with the individual, while at the same time placing responsibilities in the lap of parents; between stressing individual choice, and at the same time structuring that choice away; between decreasing direct state intervention, while increasing indirect intervention through 'The Family' and the market. Firstly, we shall consider the value of taking a life-course approach to the concept of citizenship.

A LIFE-COURSE APPROACH TO CITIZENSHIP

The concept of citizenship has neither in its original modern formulation by Marshall, nor in its more recent political and sociological manifestations, been constructed on a life-course model. The more common view is to regard citizenship in Britain as having evolved over time, with the development of its civil element in the eighteenth century, its political element in the nineteenth century, and social citizenship, the universal safety net, in the twentieth century. There have been recent attempts to broaden out this evolutionary approach. Though in theory, citizenship is universal, and the full application of citizenship would have the effect of removing social strata, inequalities do persist, because access to the rights of citizenship are structured. Marshall himself pointed out that though the desirable outcome of social citizenship was that social class inequalities would be eradicated, this was not likely to happen in practice. He did not consider other dimensions of inequality, and indeed in studies of social stratification other dimensions of inequality such as gender, race, ethnicity, and disability, have only been identified since the time that Marshall's thesis was developed. His original model of citizenship was implicitly based on the normative nuclear family, with wife and children as dependants of the male breadwinner, through whom the family's income, and also the family's rights, derived. Recently, the concept of citizenship has been applied to women, and there is more scope for considering the citizenship status of other disadvantaged groups, such as members of ethnic minorities or those who are physically or mentally handicapped. The amplification of the citizenship model in these circumstances, while increasing the scope of the concept to re-assess the position of structurally-disadvantaged groups, is still likely, however, to be based on a cross-sectional view of the social world.

It does not have to be. In practice, while all forms of stratification can be measured cross-sectionally, and it is important to identify changes at a societal level at different points in historical time, each of the many dimensions of stratification is subject to change at an individual level too. Thus, occupational class position may change during the individual biography, as well as between generations. Thus also, though sex is (largely) determined at birth, gender inequalities develop over the life course, partly as a result of domestic histories. Disability too may develop during the life course, creating a career of varying degrees of disadvantage. Even race and ethnicity may have different life-chance outcomes at different stages of the life course. A life course approach to stratification and inequality can consider individual biographies of disadvantage in this way.

The 'evolutionary' approach (Giddens, 1982) has shown how citizenship developed at the level of British society. If we apply a life-course approach to citizenship, we can examine how individuals acquire citizenship status during their life course, and indeed we could go further, and consider how citizenship changes in form over the life course – so, for example, how events such as marriage and childbirth, and post-child (or even post-marital) careers, might affect women's participation in society, or how retirement affects the rights and responsibilities of the elderly. We have focused here on young people, and have considered how and when citizenship is achieved at an individual level. There is a similarity between the three types of cases just mentioned – young people, women and the elderly – and that is in their transitional economic status, transitional from dependence to independence in the case of young people, from independence to dependence in the case of the elderly, and perhaps even more complex transitions – from independence to dependence and back to independence again – in the case of women. Just as the transition from dependence to independence may be associated with entry into full membership of society, so reversals of this transition process may be associated with loss of citizenship status. Clearly, if we want to open up citizenship to the whole population, we have to understand both how membership is stratified and how it is subject to individual and historical change.

There are several elements of citizenship which, though developed in terms of society, can be applied at the individual level too. Thus, we have suggested that the acquisition of civil, political and social rights over the life course reflects the pattern described by Marshall of the acquisition of rights in society over historical time. Thus too, we have suggested that the development of citizenship at an individual level is uneven and non-parallel, and even reversible, as Giddens (1982) and Turner (1990) have commented with regard to its development at a societal level. Finally, it is appropriate to think in terms of passive and active citizenship (Turner, 1990) at both levels.

BECOMING A CITIZEN IN BRITAIN

Like many other aspects of British life, citizenship is not embodied in any constitution, but has evolved over time. It is not always possible to fall back on precedent to make claims, and it is often possible to take away individual rights without there being any public clamour to prevent it, especially where the individual whose rights have been withdrawn lacks a collective voice of protest. Equally, of course, many of the citizenship rights in the British case have developed without very much public clamour – even the political rights of women were obtained without an outright revolution or civil war (Turner, 1990). Citizenship has evolved in very different ways, and has many different manifestations, in other countries (Turner 1990). Everywhere it may involve rights and responsibilities, but the nature of these rights and responsibilities may change. The use of the term can be negative as well as positive, and citizenship may be invoked as a means of excluding non-citizen groups, as is often the case with members of ethnic minority groups. Rights may be very localized, and associated with a city (thus the classical definition of the word citizen) or a region, rather than a nation state.

In Britain, where citizenship is at a national level, how and when do people come to be recognized as citizens, and who recognizes them as such? Given the sociological debate on citizenship, we have to assume that there is an important meaning to the concept which goes over and above the content of current political debate.

Citizenship rights and access

The basic elements of citizenship were identified by Marshall (1950) as civil rights, including property rights and the right to sign a contract, political rights, and the right to the prevailing level of health, education, standard of living in society. We have included here the right to work which formed an essential part of the Keynesian post-war economy, but have also extended the analysis to consider the rights to post-school education and training embodied in later policy initiatives, rights which are associated with citizenship as a claim to a national cultural system, but were not included in Marshall's formulation, as Turner (1990) points out.

When we begin to consider all these elements of citizenship in the context of youth, we find that they are in a complex relationship to one another. There is no question that young people become citizens in all respects when they reach the legal age of majority, or indeed at any other specified age. Eighteen may bring voting rights, and some civil rights, such as to marry or own property, and a parallel responsibility – to pay the Poll Tax – but the age does not bring full social citizenship, as we have seen. Marshall too has made the point (1973, quoted in Turner, 1990) that there is a contradiction between the political equality of the franchise and the persistence of extensive social and economic inequality – the latter being ultimately rooted in the capitalist market-place and the existence of private property. Even civil citizenship is problematic, since the rights of children and young people are still awaiting ratification in legislation. In the case of social citizenship in particular, many rights continue to be derived through parents, because of the dependent statuses in which so many young people are living.

Even where rights have been acquired, there is no reason to assume that they will be exercised – thus, even where there is eligibility for welfare provision, there may still be non-take-up of benefits; and even when young people have political rights, many studies have shown that many still do not vote, and non-voting is stratified by social class (see, for example, Jones and Wallace, 1990). Although they may have the right to participation in the electoral process or in the welfare system, exercising this right may still depend on factors such as the degree of apathy which their previous experience of the 'establishment', including the electoral process, the welfare system or the labour market, may have induced. There are indications that many young people are becoming increasingly marginalized, and excluded from participation, in the 1990s. Access to one set of rights seems to be dependent on access to another set, for example, and we have indicated how political rights may depend on housing and property rights, which are themselves dependent on an income – while an income is increasingly dependent on age and economic status.

The life-course approach shows that acquiring these rights is not only uneven and non-parallel, but also reversible – thus the loss of rights in one area can lead to the loss of rights in another, and unemployment can lead to homelessness which in its turn can lead to loss of political rights. Thus processes at an individual level reflect the problems defined by Giddens (1982) and Turner (1990) at a societal level. Giddens has argued that different rights have been the outcome of different social processes, and while political rights are the outcome of bourgeois struggle and affirm capitalism, social rights are the outcome of socialist ideology and thus present a challenge to capitalism. At an individual level too, there appears to be a tension between the different forms of citizenship. It is certainly helpful at an individual level to break down the concept of citizenship into its component parts: there are several processes (reflecting Marshall's typology of citizenship dimensions) involved in the acquisition of citizenship rights, leading separately to civil, political and social rights. Further processes then structure the access to those rights. While the rights themselves are largely acquired with age, as part of the social construction of age status, access to the rights acquired at any age is likely to be unequal and structurally determined, mainly, we have found, by economic status.

The structuring of age-status

Citizenship is associated with age status, though as we have indicated, different rights and responsibilities are broadly acquired at different ages. Individual development of citizenship status is however complex, and status depends upon more than just age qualification.

Bringing age, specifically, into the citizenship debate has some important implications, because *age* has been constructed in policy terms in a very simplistic way. There is a need for conceptual clarification. An individual's age reflects little more than a physical attribute: it tells us almost nothing about an individual's experience; if we know the individual's date of birth, we can identify their location in historical time and can see them as members of a particular cohort: this begins to indicate a little more about their experience. But it is only by locating cohort members in social and geographical space as well as in historical time, that we can really understand anything about them (Jones, 1991b). State policies intended to be 'universal', as in the case of education and training provision, show little awareness of the social context of individuals; they focus on age as a means of identifying their target population. When finer targeting is needed, age-grading has been brought into play, and this has particularly been the case where regulations determining welfare provision have been concerned. It is of course impossible to legislate for all the detail of the social and geographical context in which young people live, but there has been too great a reliance on age-graded entitlement and this can lead to gross inequalities when other social factors are ignored. It also has the result of crystallizing age status, so that all sense of the dynamic of the life course is lost. Each age, or age-grouping (for example, the common ones in training and welfare provision of 16 to 17 and 18 to 25) becomes static, and membership within each group is frozen, so that within each group, no process is involved – all sense of process is channelled into the transition from one age-grouping to another. This is clearly a very artificial formulation of age.

In policy terms, young people are a very identifiable social group, but in real terms, young people in different social contexts have vastly different life experiences. Age has been structured as one dimension of inequality, but a focus on age should not result in the overlooking of other dimensions in the overall structure of inequality.

Largely as a result of the state's emphasis on age as a structuring variable, some experiences in youth are becoming more common across the social spectrum: these include lengthening periods in education and training, less likelihood of receiving a direct income, and more state-structured dependence on their families. Some transitional economic statuses such as trainee or student have been extended, while others such as unemployed or young worker have become less common. Employment, training and education policies, backed by social security policies, have moved towards constructing just two groups of young people: trainees or students, but it is unrealistic to expect either that the move could be successful or that it would imply greater equality in youth, because, as we have seen, stratification develops within and between these statuses.

The structuring of economic independence

While the rights associated with citizenship are based on age criteria, access to many of these rights is through economic independence. From the earliest legislation creating a minimum school-leaving age and a minimum age at which children could be employed, their economic status has been structured to a large extent by the state. Over time, state control of their economic status has increased. Young people now grow up within a narrow and constricting framework of education, training and labour market structures. Ever since the idea was formed in the nineteenth century that education should be a universal right of social citizenship, the period of compulsory education has been extended. The age at which young people enter the labour market has also been increasing, but at a different rate, and now there is an intermediary period of training, further education or higher education for most people between leaving school and full-time employment. Where young people were once in the labour market, most are now absorbed into education or training provision instead. With the broadening of access to educational opportunities, a wider group of young people is beginning to gain higher qualifications, using the opportunities offered by new types of courses. Unemployment has been largely absorbed into the trainee system, though it still persists and is likely to increase. These developments could mean that new opportunities have opened up for many young people who lacked them before, though as we have indicated, the more qualifications obtained, the less highly they are valued by students and employers, and life chances are thus not necessarily improved by obtaining more certificates – equalization is therefore tempered by further stratification.

As a result of all these developments, young people are also increasingly living in an intermediate status between economic dependence and independence. Like the apprenticeships which largely preceded them, neither trainee nor student status is associated with adult income or adult responsibilities. There has never been any attempt to base the student grant on the average wage, for example, and trainee allowances are deliberately held at a level lower than average youth wages; furthermore, young people's real living costs have never been fully examined. The amount of financial support offered to young people in training and education has decreased, and financial support for unemployed 16- and 17-year-olds has now been withdrawn. Young people within all these intermediate economic statuses have thus been forced into increased economic dependence on their families.

The increasing dependence of young people on their families during the 'long transition' raises the issue of how independence can be negotiated and citizenship achieved. Young people and their families are forced into an economic relationship which neither side may want: parents may feel unable to take moral responsibility for an independent-minded adolescent child, and they may be unable to take economic responsibility if they are poor themselves; young people – young men, perhaps, especially – may be pleased to have to stay at home and continue to receive maternal care, getting their food cooked and their clothes washed; on the other hand, there are many who want to behave as adults, gain privacy in which to develop new relationships, and live independently of their parents. Because of the loss of housing and job opportunities, it has become increasingly difficult for young people to leave home, and many are forced into a child-like dependency which they may resist.

It is difficult to legislate for dependency in youth therefore. Many factors may affect both the parent's ability to support and the young person's ability to defer the attainment of adult independence. Nevertheless, Government policies are based on assumptions about the nature of family relationships and the nature of transition to adulthood. We have shown here how complex the issues of dependence and independence really are.

Citizenship by proxy?

While living as dependent children in the family setting, young people are assumed to derive their rights and benefits through their head of household: thus, they have the right to health and education, and the head of household may claim an allowance for their personal needs. At some stage, depending on the age criteria defined by legislation and regulation, young people can begin to claim rights on their own behalf. When many young people are not in practice living with two natural parents in a nuclear family situation, the assumptions underlying the notion of citizenship by proxy must be challenged. The whole ethos of this policy is further called into question by claims in the modern day for children's rights. These claims (usually, it must be said, by adults on children's behalf) are based nevertheless on the recognition of children as individuals rather than as dependants, whose rights may not necessarily be derived from their parents, and on the recognition that not all parents are able to fulfil their parental responsibilities. Citizenship by proxy is therefore problematic.

A notion of citizenship based on proxy is also difficult to put into practice. The period of transition from derived rights in childhood to the independent rights associated with adulthood presents problems for policy-makers, since benefit regulations are not geared to be based on process. It appears that they cannot therefore take account of young people's transitions to economic independence. Before 1979 there was, as we saw, the beginning of a gradual move towards paying welfare benefits directly to young people rather than to their parents on their behalf, and thus some recognition in policy thinking of young people's own rights to social citizenship. This (to our view) more enlightened approach has recently been revised again, and young people are once again not considered eligible to social citizenship in their own names. The age of majority, as far as recognition by the welfare system is concerned, has now been extended to the mid-20s.

As we argued earlier, while it may be appropriate to conceive of childhood as a dependent state, it is problematic to do so in the case of young people in their late teens. We have no evidence to show whether parents do pass on benefits to their adult children. Just as there are cases where parents do not pay their share of means-tested educational grants to their student children, and where husbands do not pass on tax benefits to their wives, so we should not assume that young people will receive benefits which their parents are given on their behalf.

Dependence and social control

We have suggested that one reason why youth has been increasingly constructed as a period of dependency is in order to exert more control over the young. This was seen as necessary following inner-city disturbances, often involving young people, in the early 1980s. One approach to the enforcement of law and order in society has been, in recent years, to stress the role of parents in controlling their children. Dependence on parents is seen as a way of placing young people under their parents' control.

The state of dependency implies an unequal power relationship between the dependants and their providers. We have suggested, however, that the gradual transition to economic independence within families, as young people begin to contribute to the household budget as well as, or instead of, drawing on household resources, is paralleled with changes in the power relationships within families – when they start to pay board money, young people improve their negotiating positions, come to be seen as more responsible and adult, and increasingly gain responsibilities associated with adulthood. The extent to which parents control their children thus varies in part according to the economic relationship between them, though this may not be the most important factor, since it is also likely to vary according to the economic status of all parties, and the other economic responsibilities of each. Policies tend not to recognize these issues.

It is the traditional view of the parent–child relationship to see the child as dependent on its parents and a subordinate member of the household. It is possible that this is a simplification, given recent change. Harris (1983) suggests that far from placing the child in a position of dependence, the modern policy assumption that parents are responsible for their children actually subverts the traditional power balance of the family. He argues that, like all producers, parents are judged by the quality of their products; thus, it is the parents' responsibility to ensure that their child learns proper social and moral behaviour. However, there is an anomaly, according to Harris (1983: 241):

> If the parent is seen as socially responsible for the character of the child; if the child's behaviour is regarded as a measure of the moral and personal worth of the parent, then the power of the child becomes enormous.

It is therefore possibly misleading to think of the dependent child as necessarily the weaker partner in the parent–child relationship.

Moves to make parents more responsible for the behaviour of their teenage children, such as to make them responsible for paying fines, all assume that young people are financially dependent on their parents, and that parents can thus control them by using financial sanctions if necessary. This does not of course work if the parents, as we suggested earlier, are financially dependent on their children instead, or if the dynamic indicated by Harris means that parents, far from gaining power *vis-à-vis* their children, are in practice losing it. If Government policy is to control young people through their dependency on their parents, then this is unlikely to work in these circumstances.

Similarly, economic status outside the household can be associated with social control. We have suggested that the introduction of YTS was linked with the emphasis that the Government of the day was placing on law and order issues. Thus, trainees (like apprentices before them) and students are both financially dependent on others, and under a degree of social control. Again, there can be financial sanctions. Financial help can be withdrawn from them if they do not comply. It is significant that the student rebellions of the 1960s were associated with a period of expansion and relative prosperity, and that students now are more likely to be having to cope with financial problems than taking part in political activities. Traineeship has taken most of the young unemployed off the streets, and we have suggested that the development of the trainee schemes was associated with the need for social control of the young after the riots in the inner cities in the early 1980s. Again, though, as we have indicated, forms of resistance have emerged within the training schemes themselves, and it would be incorrect therefore to think that policies intended to produce compliance will necessarily work. The 1991 summer spate of inner-city disturbances may be an indication that the training scheme method of social control is breaking down, in the face of increasing poverty and debt.

Choice and constraint

Where does choice exist for the young? It can be argued that there is increasing diversity and flexibility in family relations and household structures. The disassociation of sex, cohabitation or childbirth from marriage, the increase in serial partnerships – all represent a departure from what we have perceived as traditional family forms or normative patterns, and might lead to increased choice. The links between the labour market and family transitions have also changed. There is more flexibility in the labour market too, and more opportunities for post-school education and training for jobs. Consumer markets have opened up for young people. Do these new developments really lead to more choice?

We have shown here the extent to which choice is stratified in every sphere of young people's lives. Thus, opportunities are mainly available to those with the financial or cultural capital to make use of them. Many of the new choices theoretically available to young people, including new forms of household and family formation require an independent income, and access to an income is restricted. Consumer citizenship is constructed to suggest choice in the market – the ability to choose between services, or to develop personal styles. However, as Marshall (1973) has pointed out, the market works against the notion of citizenship, and so consumer citizenship is an anomaly in his terms. We have indicated here how the market creates inequality through exclusion, and even within the market, choice is clearly associated with wealth.

Responsibilities of citizenship

The imposition of dependency status on many young people who in other historical and social circumstances might be able to live independent lives, takes away adult responsibility and places young people under the legal control of their parents. Their rights to freedom and self-determination are thus restricted. So too are their responsibilities. Thus at a time when both independence and responsibilities should be increasing, they are not. Yet rights and responsibilities are inextricably linked: the civil right to property is associated with the civil responsibility to respect the property of others.

There seems to be a further dilemma here for policy-makers. How can young people learn to become responsible citizens if they are not allowed to take responsibility for themselves? In the 'New Right's' own discussion about citizenship, it has been argued that power should be decentralized and civic responsibilities become the responsibility of all. We would argue that this process of democratization should be extended to young people too. If they are to gain any sense of the obligations of citizenship in our society, they must be treated as citizens and granted rights of citizenship.

There are therefore several dilemmas for policy-makers. While it may be desirable to construct youth as a period of dependence on parents, rather than on the state, thus in theory at least achieving the twin goals of reducing the social security budget and increasing law and order, there are various reasons why this policy cannot work. As we have indicated, dependency is problematic, it is associated with resistance rather than social control, and power relations in the family can also be complex. Furthermore, it becomes increasingly untenable for rhetoric to stress citizenship responsibilities on the one hand,

and to withdraw them from young people on the other hand. Young people are the civil, political and social citizens of the future, and if they are to fulfil the obligations of citizenship as adults, they must surely be encouraged to learn these responsibilities when young.

FUTURE DIRECTIONS

We have argued that the sociology of youth needs to take account of holism, process, diversity and inequality, and have used the concept of citizenship as a way of capturing these issues. The sterile study of concepts such as youth and adulthood without concern about their meanings in the real world adds nothing to our understanding, and can be detrimental to young people. Social policy needs to be informed by good and reliable research. It seems to us too that by bringing the concept of citizenship into the study of youth, we may begin to develop an interesting framework for cross-national comparative research.

Improving policies

There is scope for improving policies for young people and dealing at the same time with some of the dilemmas we have indicated. There are two basic changes which we would advocate. The first is to take a more holistic approach to young people's needs; the second is to focus more on process in youth, but rely less on age as a structuring variable.

It is clearly necessary to recognize age inequalities in society, and also to determine some, albeit arbitrary, age at which people can derive certain rights in law. However, as we have argued, when policies are based on finer age-grading, they tend to lose all sense of the processes running through the life course, and also of the different life-course patterns of different social groupings. We would argue therefore that recent legislation basing assessed need on age, rather than on social circumstances, should be revised.

In order to be able to do this successfully, it is also important to take a holistic approach to young people's lives, and we would argue here for an integrated policy approach. Davies (1986) has suggested that a new concerted 'youth policy' has already emerged, but this has so far taken a negative form. We argue instead for integrated policies to take a positive and constructive approach, and indeed it is becoming increasingly apparent that the current problems affecting young people – problems of homelessness, joblessness and poverty (which are likely to continue well into the 1990s) – can only be solved through an integrated policy. Thus, the problem of homelessness cannot be approached without consideration of employment and income opportunities, and without recognition that access to all of these is unequal. We are not arguing here for a Ministry of Youth, which could lead to increased marginalization of the young, but for more discussion between government departments, more joint funding, more combined intelligence, in a way that current bureaucratic structures tend to make difficult.

In these ways, it would be possible to gain a greater understanding of young people's needs, and in particular of the financial cost to individuals and their families of growing up and participating as citizens in society. This will also involve further research on young people's economic circumstances, their financial outgoings and the relevance and importance of an independent income in youth.

A framework for comparative studies

We have focused here on youth in a British context. Young people are also becoming citizens of a new and rapidly transforming Europe. Their rights and responsibilities in this context could be a focus for future research. At present, citizenship status is defined by nation-state structures and although the trends we have described (new patterns of family formation, household formation and extended dependency in education and training, increasing consumer power) are also common, or even more marked, in other European countries, citizenship in youth may still take many different national forms. Turner's (1990) typology, linked with our own discussion, might provide the basis for further work in this area.

The concepts we have outlined could therefore be used as a starting-point from which to explore the position of young people in different national contexts, for example in terms of their living situations and extent of dependence on family or state provision. There could be studies which identify the degree of consistency in the forms of citizenship rights and responsibilities across national frontiers. Young people's biographies could be compared in terms of the acquisition over the early life course of citizenship rights, and the differing ways in which access to these rights is structured in different societies. The analysis would involve clarification of the concepts of dependence and independence in other national contexts. It seems to us that studies of this kind might prove more fruitful ways of understanding how young people become adult in different countries, because they will involve exploring how the concepts of youth and adulthood are constructed in practice.

APPENDIX – CHRONOLOGY

OF MAIN EVENTS

PRE-1940

1833   Factory Act. Restricted age at which children could work in factories.

1908   Old Age Pensions Act. Compulsory pensions insurance for workers.

1911   National Insurance Act. Compulsory unemployment insurance for shipbuilders, engineering workers and building workers aged 16–70 years.

1918   Education Act. School leaving age raised to 14 years.

1921   Unemployed Workers (Dependants) Act. Temporary provision for dependants of workers introduced as 'winter relief'.

1922   Unemployment Insurance Act. Made provision for dependants permanent.

1925   Widows and Orphans Act. Benefits for bereaved dependants introduced.

1930   National Insurance entry age reduced to 15; claiming age 16 years.

1934   National Insurance entry age reduced to 14; claiming age 16 years.

1938   Spens Report. Recommended school leaving age be raised to 16 years.

1940–1979

1942   Beverage Plan Report.

1944   Education Act. School leaving age raised to 15 years.

1945   Family Allowances Act.

1959   Crowther Report. Recommended provision of Further
         Education for 15–18-year-olds, especially school leavers.
1963   Robbins Report. Recommended extension of Higher
         Education as universal provision for all with the ability.
1964   National Insurance Act. Extended family allowance for
         dependants up to 19 years.
1964   Creation of mandatory Local Authority maintenance grants
         for those accepted for a place in Higher Education.
1966   Ministry of Social Security Act. National Assistance replaced
         by Supplementary Benefit.
1967   Latey Committee Report (lowering of age of majority from
         21 to 18 years).
1972   School leaving age changed to 16 years: (ROSLA).
1977   Child Benefit introduced (replaced Child Tax Allowance
         and Family Allowance).
1977   Holland Report. Youth Opportunities Programme introduced.
1979   Election of 'New Right' Conservative Government.

1980–1985

1980   Social Security Act. Young people disadvantaged in
         claiming benefit.
1982   Social Security and Housing Benefit Act.
1983   Youth Training Scheme introduced.
1983   Contribution to 'board' in non-householder's benefit
         withdrawn from 16–17-year-olds.
1984   Changes in Housing Benefit Regulations (non-dependant
         deductions from parents increased).
1984   Contribution to 'board' in non-householders benefit
         withdrawn from 18–20-year-olds.
1985   Board and Lodgings Regulations. Introduced time limits
         and rent ceilings for under-25's.
1985   Fowler Review of Social Security.

1986–1988

1986   YTS extended to two years.
1986   Wages Act. Under-25's removed from protection of Wages
         Councils.
1986   Social Security Act. Abolished Supplementary Benefit,
         introduced Income Support; reduced benefit levels for
         young people; benefits payable in arrears.
1986   Contribution to 'board' in non-householders benefit
         withdrawn from 21–24-year-olds.

1986/7 Student entitlement to Income Support during short
        vacations withdrawn
1987   Government White Paper on Higher Education.
1987   Householder rates of benefit abolished for those under 26
        years.
1987   Local Government Finance Act. Proposed introduction of
        Community Charge/Poll Tax in Scotland.
1988   Social Security Act. Withdrew eligibility for benefit from
        most 16–17-year-olds; YTS made compulsory for
        unemployed 16–17-year-olds; Householder/non-
        householder distinction abolished, eligibility for adult rate
        raised to 25 years.
1988   Housing Act. Encouraged the de-regulation of rents in the
        private-rented sector.
1988   Local Government Finance Act (proposed introduction of
        Community Charge/Poll Tax in England and Wales).
1988   Employment Act. Introduced bridging allowances for YTS
        trainees.
1988   Student eligibility for Housing Benefit restricted.

1989–1991

1989   Board and lodging time limits removed; Housing Benefit to
        cover cost of lodgings or hostels.
1989   Severe Hardship payments introduced for 16–17-year-olds.
1989   Children's Act (England and Wales). Rights of children within
        families recognized and made more explicit. Local authorities
        must report on any 16–17-year-olds in serious need.
1989   Social Security Act. Unemployment benefit made
        dependent on claimant actively seeking work.
1989   Employment Act. Lifted working restrictions on young
        people (including shift work and dangerous machinery).
1989   Income Support 18–24 rate paid to 16–17-year-olds if they
        'have good reason' for living away from home.
1990   Introduction of student 'top-up' loans. Withdrawal of
        Housing Benefit from students.
1990   YTS renamed Youth Training.
1990   Government initiatives on homelessness – Direct Access
        hostels scheme set up; allowance for rents payable in advance.
1991   Government White Paper on Higher Education.
        Recommended expansion of student numbers.
1991   Student entitlement to Income Support during long
        vacations withdrawn.

REFERENCES

Abbott, P. and Sapsford, R. (1990). 'Health visiting: policing the family?' in P. Abbott and C. Wallace, (eds) *The Sociology of the Caring Professions*. Basingstoke, Falmer.

Abbott, P. and Wallace, C. (eds)(1990). *The Sociology of the Caring Professions*. Basingstoke, Falmer.

Abbott, P. and Wallace, C. (1991). *The New Right and the Family: Implications for Social Policy in Britain and the USA*. London, Pluto Press.

Abrams, P. (1961). *The Teenage Consumer*. London, London Press Exchange.

Aggleton, P. (1987). *Rebels without a Cause*. Basingstoke, Falmer.

Ainley, P. (1988). *From School to YTS: Education and Training in England and Wales 1944–1987*. Milton Keynes, Open University Press.

Ainley, P. and Corney, M. (1990). *Training for the Future: The Rise and Fall of the Manpower Services Commission*. London, Cassell.

Allan, G. (1985). *Family Life: Domestic Roles and Social Organization*. Oxford, Basil Blackwell.

Allan, G. and Crow, G. (1988). 'Constructing the domestic sphere: the emergence of the modern home in post-war Britain'. Paper presented at the BSA Annual Conference, University of Edinburgh, March.

Allatt, P. (1986). 'The young unemployed: independence and identity' in B. Pashley, (ed.) *Unemployment and the Transition to Adulthood: Needs and Responses*. Papers in *Social Policy and Professional Studies, 4*, University of Hull.

Allatt, P. and Yeandle, S. (1986). "It's not fair is it?" Youth unemployment, family relations and the social contract' in S. Allen, *et al*. (eds) *The Experience of Unemployment*. London, Macmillan.

Althusser, L. (1971). 'Ideology and ideological state apparatuses' in *Lenin and Philosophy and Other Essays*. London, New Left Books.

Anderson, M. (1971). *Family Structure in Nineteenth Century Lancashire*. Cambridge, Cambridge University Press.

Anderson, M. (1980). *Approaches to the History of the Western Family 1500–1914*. London, Macmillan.

Anderson, M. (1983). 'What is new about the modern family: an historical perspective' in *The Family*. British Society for Population Studies Conference, University of Bath, 14–16 September 1983, *OPCS Occasional Paper 31*. London, OPCS.

Ashton, D.N. and Field, D. (1976). *Young Workers*. London, Hutchinson.

Ashton, D.N. and Lowe, G. (eds)(1990). *Making Their Way: School to Work Transitions in Britain and Canada*. Milton Keynes, Open University Press.

Ashton, D.N. and Maguire, M. (1982). 'Youth in the Labour Market', *Research Paper No. 34*. London, Department of Employment.

Ashton, D.N., Maguire, M. and Spilsbury, M. (1987). 'Labour market segmentation and the structure of youth labour markets' in P. Brown and D.N. Ashton, (eds) *Education, Unemployment and Labour Markets*. Lewes, Falmer.

Bagguley, P. (1991). 'Post-Fordism and the enterprise culture: flexibility, autonomy and changes in economic organisation' in N. Abercrombie and R. Keat, (eds) *Enterprise Culture*. London, Routledge.

Barbalet, J.M. (1988). *Citizenship*. Milton Keynes, Open University Press.

Barr, N. (1989). 'The White Paper on student loans' *Journal of Social Policy*, 18(3), 409–18.

Barrett, M. and McIntosh, M. (1980). *The Anti-Social Family*. London, Verso.

Bates, I. (1989a). 'Designer careers: an initial analysis focusing on the influence of family background, gender and vocational training in female careers.' *ESRC 16–19 Initiative Occasional Paper 23*. London, SSRU, City University.

Bates, I. (1989b). 'No bleeding, whining minnies: The role of YTS in class and gender reproduction'. *ESRC 16–19 Initiative Occasional Paper 19*. London, SSRU, City University.

Baxter, J.L. (1975). 'The chronic job changer: a study of youth unemployment' *Social and Economic Administration*, 9 (3), 184–206.

Beck, U. (1986). *Risikogesellschaft: Auf dem Weg in eine andere Moderne*. Frankfurt, Suhrkamp.

Beck, U. (1987). 'Beyond status and class' in W. Mega, *et al.* (eds) *Modern German Sociology*. Columbia, Columbia University Press.

Beechey, V. (1977). *Capital and Class*, 3, 45–66.

Bell, C. (1968). *Middle Class Families: Social and Geographical Mobility*. London, Routledge and Kegan Paul.

Berger (1963). 'Adolescence and beyond' *Social Problems*, 10, 394–408.

Bernardes, J. (1986). 'In search of "The Family" – analysis of the 1981 United Kingdom Census data: a research note' *Sociological Review*, 34(4), 828–36.

Bertaux, D. (1981). 'From the life history approach to the transformation of sociological practice' in D. Bertaux, (ed.) *Biography and Society*. London, Sage.

Bloss, T., Frickey, A. and Godard, F. (1990). 'Cohabiter, décohabiter, recohabiter: itinéraires de générations de femmes' *Revue Française de Sociologie*, XXXI-4, 553–72.

Bourdieu, P. and Passeron, J.D. (1977). *Reproduction in Education, Society and Culture*. London, Sage.

Bowles, S. and Gintis, H. (1976). *Schooling in Capitalist America: Educational Reform and the Contradictions of Economic Life*. London, Routledge and Kegan Paul.

Brake, M. (1980). *The Sociology of Youth Culture and Youth Sub-cultures*. London, Routledge and Kegan Paul.

Brannen, J. and Wilson, G. (eds) (1987). *Give and Take in Families*. London, Allen and Unwin.

Brown, C. (1984). *Black and White Britain*. Aldershot, Gower.

Brown, P. and Lauder, H. (1992). 'Education, economy and society: an introduction to a new agenda' in P. Brown and H. Lauder, (eds) *Education and Economic Survival: From Fordism to Post-Fordism*. London, Routledge.

Burgoyne, J. and Clarke, D. (1984). *Making a Go of It: A Study of Step Families in Sheffield*. London, Routledge and Kegan Paul.

Burton, P., Forrest, R. and Stewart, M. (1989). 'Urban environment, accommodation, social cohesion: the implications for young people'. Consolidated Report. University of Bristol, SOAS.

Buswell, C. (1986). 'Employment processes and youth training' in S. Walker and L. Barton, (eds) *Youth, Unemployment and Schooling*. Milton Keynes, Open University Press.

Bynner, J. (1990). 'Transition to work: results from a longitudinal study of young people in four British labour markets' in D.N. Ashton and G. Lowe, (eds) *Making Their Way: Education, Training and the Labour Market in Britain and Canada*. Milton Keynes, Open University Press.

Carling, A. (1992). 'Rational choice and household division' in C. Marsh and S. Arber, (eds) *Families and Households: Divisions and Change*. Basingstoke, Macmillan.

Carter, M.P. (1962). *Home, School and Work*. London, Pergamon Press.

Carter, M.P. (1966). *Into Work*. Penguin, Harmondsworth.

Carter, M.P. (1975). 'Teenage workers: a second chance at eighteen?' in P. Brannen, (ed.) *Entering the World of Work: Some Sociological Perspectives*. London, Department of Employment.

Chandler, E.J. and Wallace, C. (1990). 'Some alternatives in youth training: franchise and corporatist models' in D. Gleeson, (ed.) *Training and its Alternatives*. Milton Keynes, Open University Press.

Cherry, N. (1976). 'Persistent job changing – is it a problem?' *Journal of Occupational Psychology*, 49, 203–21.

Clark, A. and Hirst, M. (1989). 'Disability in adulthood: ten year follow-up of young people with disabilities' *Disability, Handicap and Society*, 4(3), 271–83.

Clarke, J. and Critcher, C. (1985). *The Devil Makes Work: Leisure in Capitalist Britain*. London, Macmillan.

Cohen, P. (1972). 'Subcultural conflicts and working class community' in M. Hammersley, and P. Woods, (eds)(1976) *The Process of Schooling*. London, Routledge and Kegan Paul.

Coleman, J.S. (1961). *The Adolescent Society*. New York, Free Press.

Coleman, R. (1986). 'Social standing and income packaging' in L. Rainwater, *et al.* (eds) *Income Packaging and the Welfare State*. Oxford, Clarendon Press.

Corrigan, P. (1979). *Schooling the Smash Street Kids*. London, Macmillan.

Corrigan, P. (1989). 'Gender and the gift: the case of the family clothing economy' *Sociology*, 23(4), 513–534.

Cross, M. (1987). 'A cause for concern: ethnic minority youth and vocational training policy'. Policy paper, in *Ethnic Relations 9*, ESRC Centre for Research into Ethnic Relations, University of Warwick.

Cross, M. and Smith, D.I. (1987). *Black Youth Futures: Ethnic Minorities and the Youth Training Scheme*. Leicester, National Youth Bureau.

Cunningham-Burley, S. (1985). 'Constructing grandparenthood: anticipating appropriate action' *Sociology*, 19(3), 421–36.

Cusack, S. and Roll, J. (1985). *Families Rent Apart*. London, Child Poverty Action Group.

Dale, A. (1987). 'The effect of life cycle on three dimensions of stratification' in A. Bryman, *et al.* (eds) *Rethinking the Life Cycle*. London, Macmillan.

Dale, A. (1988). 'Part-time work among young people in Britain'. *ESRC 16–19 Initiative Occasional Paper 3*. London, SSRU, City University.

Dale, R. (1985). *Education, Training and Employment. Towards a New Vocationalism?* Milton Keynes, Open University Press.

David, M. (1991). 'Putting on an act for children?' in M. Maclean and D. Groves, (eds) *Women's Issues in Social Policy*. London, Routledge.

Davies, B. (1986). *Threatening Youth: Towards a National Youth Policy*. Milton Keynes, Open University Press.

Deem, R. (1986). *All Work and No Play? Sociology of Women and Leisure*. Milton Keynes, Open University Press.

Department of Environment (1981). *Single and Homeless*. London, HMSO.

Donzelot, J. (1979). *The Policing of Families*. London, Hutchinson.

Eisenstadt, S.N. (1956). 'From generation to generation' reprinted in H. Silverstein, (ed.) (1973). *The Sociology of Youth: Evolution and Revolution*. New York, Macmillan.

Erikson, E.H. (1968). *Identity, Youth and Crisis*. New York, Norton.

Ermisch, J. and Overton, E. (1984). *Minimal Household Units: A New Perspective on the Demographic and Economic Analysis of Household Formation*. London, Policy Studies Institute.

Evans-Pritchard, E.E. (1951). *Kinship and Marriage among the Nuer*. Oxford, Oxford University Press.

Featherstone, M. (1990). 'Perspectives on consumer culture' *Sociology*, 24(1), 5–22.

Fevre, R. (1987). 'Subcontracting in steel' *Work, Employment and Society*, 1(4), 507–27.

Finch, J. (1989). *Family Obligations and Social Change*. Cambridge, Polity Press.

Finn, D. (1987). *Training Without Jobs: New deals and broken promises*. London, Macmillan.

Flandrin, J-L. (1979). *Families in Former Times: Kinship, Household and Sexuality* (trans. R. Southern). Cambridge, Cambridge University Press.

Fogelman, K. (ed.) (1976). *Britain's Sixteen Year Olds*. London, National Children's Bureau.

Fraser, N. (1990). 'Rethinking the public sphere: a contribution to the critique of actually existing democracy'. *International Sociological Association World Congress*, Madrid, July.

Friedenberg, E.Z. (1973). 'The vanishing adolescent' in H. Silverstein, (ed.) *The Sociology of Youth: Evolution and Revolution*. New York, Macmillan.

Frith, S. (1978). *The Sociology of Rock*. London, Constable.

Frith, S. (1984). *The Sociology of Youth*. Ormskirk, Causeway Press.

Furlong, A. (1990). 'A decade of decline: social class and post-school destinations of minimum age school leavers in Scotland 1977–1987' in C. Wallace and M. Cross, (eds) *Youth in Transition: The Sociology of Youth and Youth Policy*. Basingstoke, Falmer.

Gaiser, W. (1991). 'Prolongation of the youth-phase in the Federal Republic of Germany: the life situation and coping strategies of young people and the consequences for social policy' *Youth and Policy*, 32, 34–8.

Galland, O. (1990). 'Un nouvel âge de la vie' *Revue Française de Sociologie*, XXXI-4, 529-51.

Giddens, A. (1982). *Profiles and Critiques in Social Theory*. London, Macmillan.

Giddens, A. (1991). *Modernity and Self-Identity*. Cambridge, Polity Press.

Gillis, J.R. (1985). *For Better or Worse: British Marriage 1600 to the Present*. Oxford, Oxford University Press.

Ginzberg, E. *et al.* (1951). *Occupational Choice*. New York, Columbia University Press.

Gleeson, D. (ed.) (1987). *TVEI and Secondary Education: A Critical Appraisal*. Milton Keynes, Open University Press.

Goldthorpe, J. (1980). *Social Mobility and Class Structure in Modern Britain*. Oxford, Clarendon Press.

Goldthorpe, J. *et al.* (1969). *The Affluent Worker in the Class Structure*. Cambridge, Cambridge University Press.

Goode, W. (1970). *The Family*, 2nd edn (1982). New Jersey, Prentice-Hall.

Graham, H. (1983). 'Caring: a labour of love' in J. Finch and D. Groves, (eds) *A Labour of Love: Women, Work and Caring*. London, Routledge and Kegan Paul.

Greve, J. and Currie, E. (1990). *Homelessness in Britain*. York, Joseph Rowntree Foundation.

Griffin, C. (1985). *Typical Girls?* London, Routledge and Kegan Paul.

The Guardian (1983). 'Leaked discussion of the Central Policy Review Staff', 17 February 1983.

Hall, G. Stanley (1904). *Adolescence*. New York, Appleton.

Hall, S. and Jefferson, T. (eds) (1976). *Resistance through Rituals*. London, Hutchinson.

Halsey, A.H., Heath, A.F. and Ridge, J.M. (1980). *Origins and Destinations: Family, Class and Education in Modern Britain*. Oxford, Clarendon Press.

Halsey, A.H. (ed.)(1988). *British Social Trends since 1900: A Guide to the Changing Social Structure of Britain*. London, Macmillan.

Hareven, T.K. (1982). *Family Time and Industrial Time*. Cambridge, Cambridge University Press.

Harris, C.C. (1983). *The Family and Industrial Society*. London, George Allen and Unwin.

Harris, N.S. (1989). *Social Security for Young People*. Aldershot, Avebury.

Harrison, M.L. (1991). 'Citizenship, consumption and rights: a comment on B.S. Turner's theory of citizenship' *Sociology*, 25(2), 209–13.

Hartmann, J. (1987). 'The impact of new technologies on youth–parent relations in contemporary societies: the trend for individualization'. Paper presented to the CFR/CYR International Seminar *Young People and their Families*, Freising, Munich.

Hayes, L. (1991). 'Young people, the family and obligations'. PhD thesis, Department of Applied Social Science, University of Lancaster.

Hebdige, D. (1979). *Sub-culture: The Meaning of Style*. London, Methuen.

Heinz, W. (1987). 'The transition from school to work in crisis: coping with threatening unemployment' *Journal of Adolescent Research*, 2(2), 127–41.

Heinz, W. *et al.* (1987). *Hauptsache eine Lehrstelle. Jugendliche vor den Huerden des Arbeitsmarkt.* Weinheim, Deutsche Studien Verlag.

Heinz, W. *et al.* (1988). *Status Passages and the Life Course.* Project description, SFB 186, Bremen, Postfach 330440.

Hermanns, M. (1987). 'Developments in family and youth law indicating and favouring changes in the relationship between young people and their parents'. Paper presented to the CFR/CYR International Seminar *Young People and their Families*, Freising, Munich.

Hewitt, R. (1988). *White Talk, Black Talk: Inter-racial Friendships and Communication amongst Adolescents.* Cambridge, Cambridge University Press.

Hoggart, R. (1958). *The Uses of Literacy.* Harmondsworth, Penguin.

Holland Report (1977). *Young People and Work.* Sheffield, Manpower Services Commission.

Howieson, C. (1990). 'Beyond the gate: work experience and part-time work among secondary school pupils in Scotland' *British Journal of Education and Work*, 3(3), 49–61.

Hutson, S. and Cheung, W-Y (1992). 'Saturday jobs: sixth-formers in the Labour Market' in C. Marsh and S. Arber, (eds) *Families and Households: Divisions and Change.* London, Macmillan.

Hutson, S. and Jenkins, R. (1987). 'Coming of age in South Wales' in D. Ashton and P. Brown, (eds) *Education and Economic Life.* Brighton, Falmer.

Hutson, S. and Jenkins, R. (1989). *Taking the Strain: Families, Unemployment and the Transition to Adulthood.* Milton Keynes, Open University Press.

Hutson, S. and Liddiard, M. (1991). *Young and Homeless in Wales.* Department of Sociology and Anthropology, University College, Swansea.

Hutton, S. (1991). 'The effects of unemployment on the early years of adult life: evidence from national survey data'. SPRU, University of York.

Jamieson, L. (1986). 'Limited resources limiting conventions: working class mothers and daughters in urban Scotland *c.*1890–1925' in J. Lewis, (ed.) *Labour and Love: Women's Experiences of Work and Family 1850–1940.* Oxford, Basil Blackwell.

Jamieson, L. (1987). 'Theories of family development and the experience of being brought up' *Sociology*, 21(4), 591–607.

Jamieson, L. and Corr, H. (1990). 'Earning your keep: self-reliance and family obligation', *ESRC 16–19 Initiative Occasional Paper 30.* London, SSRU, City University.

Jenkins, R. (1983). *Lads, Citizens and Ordinary Kids.* London, Routledge and Kegan Paul.

Jenkins, R. *et al.* (1983). 'Information in the labour market: the impact of recession' *Sociology*, 17(2), 260–67.

Jones, G. (1986). 'Youth in the social structure: transitions to adulthood and their Stratification by Class and Gender'. PhD thesis, University of Surrey.

Jones, G. (1987a). 'Young workers in the class structure' *Work, Employment and Society*, 1(4), 487–508.

Jones, G. (1987b). 'Leaving the parental home: an analysis of early housing careers' *Journal of Social Policy*, 16(1), 49–74.

Jones, G. (1988). 'Integrating process and structure in the concept of youth' *Sociological Review*, 36(4), 706–31.

Jones, G. (1990a). *Household Formation among Young Adults in Scotland.* Edinburgh, Scottish Homes.

Jones, G. (1990b). 'Marriage partners and their class trajectories' in G. Payne and P. Abbott, (eds) *The Social Mobility of Women*. London, Falmer.

Jones, G. (1991a). 'The cost of living in the parental home', *Youth and Policy*, 32, 19–29.

Jones, G. (1991b). 'The cohort in time and space' *Bulletin de Methodologie Sociologique*, 30, 44–54.

Jones, G. (1992). 'Short-term reciprocity in parent–child economic exchanges' in C. Marsh and S. Arber, (eds) *Household and Family: Divisions and Change*. Basingstoke, Macmillan.

Jones, G. and Wallace, C. (1990). 'Beyond individualization: what sort of social change?' in L. Chisholm, *et al.* (eds) *Childhood, Youth and Social Change: A Comparative Perspective*. London, Falmer.

Kelvin, P. and Jarrett, J. E. (1985). *Unemployment. Its Social Psychological Effects*. Cambridge, Cambridge University Press.

Kerckhoff, A. (1990). *Getting Started: Entering the Adult World in Great Britain*. Denver, CO, Westview Press.

Kertzer, D. I. (1983). 'Generation as a sociological problem' *Annual Review of Sociology*, 9, 125–49.

Kiernan, K. (1983). 'The structure of families today: continuity or change?' in *The Family*. British Society for Population Studies Conference, University of Bath, 14–16 September 1983, *OPCS Occasional Paper 31*. London, OPCS.

Kiernan, K. (1985). 'A demographic analysis of first marriages in England and Wales: 1950–1985', *CPS Research Paper 85-1*. London, Centre for Population Studies.

Kiernan, K. and Wicks, M. (1990). *Family Change and Future Policy*. London, Family Policy Studies Centre (with Joseph Rowntree Foundation).

Kirk, D. *et al.* (1991). *Excluding Youth: Poverty among Young People Living Away from Home*. Edinburgh Centre for Social Welfare Research, University of Edinburgh.

Komarovsky, M. (1967). *Blue Collar Marriage*. New York, Vintage Books.

Land, H. (1989). 'The construction of dependency' in M. Bulmer, *et al.* (eds) *The Goals of Social Policy*. London, Unwin Hyman.

Lash, S. (1990). *The Sociology of Post-Modernism*. London, Routledge.

Lash, S. and Urry, J. (1987). *The End of Organised Capitalism*. Oxford, Polity Press.

Laslett, P. (1971). *The World We Have Lost*. London, Methuen.

Laslett, P. (1972). 'Mean household size in England since the sixteenth century' in P. Laslett and W. Wall, (eds) *Household and Family in Past Time*. Cambridge, Cambridge University Press.

Latey Committee Report (1967). Report of the Committee on the Age of Majority, Cmnd 3342. London, HMSO.

Layard, R., King, J. and Moser, C. (1969). *The Impact of Robbins*. Harmondsworth, Penguin.

Lee, D.J. (1990). 'Surrogate employment, surrogate labour markets and the development of training policies in the eighties' in C. Wallace and M. Cross, (eds) *Youth in Transition*. Basingstoke, Falmer.

Lee, D. *et al.* (1990). *Scheming for Youth: A Study of YTS in the Enterprise Culture*. Milton Keynes, Open University Press.

Lees, S. (1986). *Losing Out: Sexuality and Adolescent Girls*. London, Hutchinson.

Leonard, D. (1980). *Sex and Generation: A Study of Courtship and Weddings*. London, Tavistock.

Liddiard, M. and Hutson, S. (1991). 'Youth homelessness in Wales' in C. Wallace and M. Cross, (eds) *Youth in Transition: The Sociology of Youth and Youth Policy*. London, Falmer.

Lister, R. (1990). 'Women, economic dependency and citizenship' *Journal of Social Policy*, 19(4), 445–67.

Lister, R. (1991). 'Citizenship engendered' *Critical Social Policy*, 32, 65–71.

MacDonald, M. (1980). 'Socio-cultural reproduction and women's education' in R. Deem, (ed.) *Schooling for Women's Work*. London, Routledge and Kegan Paul.

MacDonald, R. and Coffield, F. (1991), *Risky Business? Youth and the Enterprise Culture*. London, Falmer Press.

MacFarlane, A. (1978). *The Origins of English Individualism: The Family, Property and Social Transition*. Oxford, Basil Blackwell.

MacLennan, E., Fitz, J. and Sullivan, J. (1985). *Working Children*. Pamphlet No. 34, Low Pay Unit.

McRae, S. (1986). *Cross-Class Families*. Oxford, Clarendon Press.

McRobbie, A. (1991). *Feminism and Youth Culture*. London, Macmillan.

McRobbie, A. and Garber, J. (1976). 'Girls and subcultures: an exploration' in S. Hall and T. Jefferson, (eds) *Resistance through Rituals*. London, Hutchinson.

Maizels, J. (1970). *Adolescent Needs and the Transition from School to Work*. University of London, Athlone Press.

Makeham, P. (1980). 'Youth unemployment. An examination of the evidence on youth unemployment using national statistics'. Department of Employment Research Paper no. 10. Department of Employment, London.

Mannheim, K. (1927). 'The problem of generations' in P. Kecskemeti, (ed./ trans.) (1952). *Essays on the Sociology of Knowledge*. London, Routledge and Kegan Paul.

Mansfield, P. and Collard, J. (1988). *The Beginning of the Rest of Your Life? A Portrait of Newly-wed Marriage*. Basingstoke, Macmillan.

Marcuse, H. (1968). *One Dimensional Man*. London, Sage.

Marketing Directions Ltd (1988). *Youth Facts*. Market Directions Ltd, 1 Palace Gate, Hampton Court Road, London.

Marshall, T.H. (1950). *Citizenship and Social Class and Other Essays*. Cambridge, Cambridge University Press.

Marshall, T.H. (1952). *Citizenship and Social Class*. Cambridge, Cambridge University Press.

Marshall, T.H. (1973). *Class, Citizenship and Social Development*. Westport, CN, Greenwood Press.

Marsland, D. (1986). 'Young people, the family and the state' in D. Anderson and G. Dawson, (eds) *Family Matters*. London, Social Affairs Unit.

Martin, B. (1983). *The Sociology of Contemporary Cultural Change*. Oxford, Basil Blackwell.

Massey, D. and Meagan, R.A. (1982). *The Anatomy of Job Loss: The How, Why and Where of Employment Decline*. London, Methuen.

Mathews, R. (1986). 'Out of house, out of home? Board and Lodgings Regulations' *Poverty*, 62, 15–16.

Mayall, B. (1990). 'The division of labour in early child care – mothers and others' *Journal of Social Policy*, 19(3), 299–330.

Mead, L. (1986). *Beyond Entitlement: The Social Obligations of Citizenship*. New York, Free Press, Macmillan.

Mead, M. (1943). *Coming of Age in Samoa*. Harmondsworth, Penguin Books.

Midwinter, A. and Monaghan, C. (1990). 'The measurement and analysis of rural deprivation'. Report prepared for the Convention of Scottish Local Authorities, University of Strathclyde.

Miller, S. (1989). 'Thatcherism, citizenship and the Poll Tax' in M. Brenton and C. Ungerson, (eds) *Social Policy Review 1988–9*. London, Longmans.

Millward, N. (1968). 'Family status and behaviour at work' *Sociological Review*, 16, 149–64.

Moos, M. (1983). 'The training myth: a critique of the government's response to youth unemployment and its impact on Further Education' in D. Gleeson, (ed.) *Youth Training and the Search for Work*. London, Routledge.

Morgan, D.H.J. (1985). *The Family, Politics and Social Theory*. London, Routledge and Kegan Paul.

MORI (1991). 'A survey of 16 and 17 year old applicants for severe hardship payments'. Research study conducted for Department of Social Security, July.

Morris, L. (1987). 'The life cycle and the labour market in Hartlepool' in A. Bryman, *et al.* (eds) *Rethinking the Life Cycle*. Basingstoke, Macmillan.

Morris, L. (1990). *The Workings of the Household: A US–UK Comparison*. Cambridge, Polity Press.

Mungham, G. and Pearson, G. (eds) (1976). *Working Class Youth Cultures*. London, Routledge and Kegan Paul.

Murphy, M. and Sullivan, O. (1986). 'Unemployment, housing and household structure among young adults' *Journal of Social Policy*, 15(2), 205–22.

Murray, C. (1986). *Losing Ground: American Social Policy 1950–1980*. New York, Basic Books.

Murray, C. (1990). *The Emerging British Underclass*. London, IEA Health and Welfare Unit.

Musgrove, F. (1974). *Ecstasy and Holiness: Counter Culture and the Open Society*. London, Methuen.

Myles, J. (1991). 'Is there a post-Fordist life course?' Paper presented to the *Symposium on Status Passages and their Institutional Regulation*. University of Bremen.

National Opinion Poll. (1987) *Financial Research Survey*, April–September.

New Earnings Surveys (1970–1990). London, Central Statistical Office, HMSO.

Newson, J. and Newson, E. (1976). *Seven Years Old in the Home Environment*. Harmondsworth, Penguin Books.

Ogus, A.I. (1982) 'Great Britain' in P.A. Koehler and H. F. Zacher (eds) *The Evolution of Social Insurance 1881–1981*. London, Francis Pinter.

Olk, T. (1988). 'Gesellschaftstheoretische Ansaetze in der Jugendforschung' in H. H. Krueger, (ed.) *Handbuch der Jugendforschung*. Opladen, Leske und Budrich.

O'Mahoney, B. (1988). *A Capital Offence: The Plight of Young Single Homeless in London*. London, Routledge.

Owen, S. (1987). 'Household production and economic efficiency: arguments for and against domestic specialization' *Work, Employment and Society*, 1(2), 157–78.

Pahl, J. (1983). 'The allocation of money and the structuring of inequality within marriage' *Sociological Review*, 31, 237–62.

Pahl, J. (1989). *Money and Marriage*. London, Macmillan.

Pahl, J. (1991). 'Money, power and marriage' in P. Abbott and C. Wallace, (eds) *Gender, Power and Sexuality*. London, Macmillan.

Pahl, R.E. (1984). *Divisions of Labour*. Oxford, Basil Blackwell.

Pahl, R.E. and Wallace, C.D. (1988). 'Neither angels in marble nor rebels in red: privatization and working-class consciousness' in D. Rose, (ed.) *Social Stratification and Economic Change*. London, Hutchinson.

Parsons, K. (1991). 'Trainers, tutors and the YTS environment' in C. Wallace and M. Cross, (eds) *Youth in Transition: The Sociology of Youth and Youth Policy*. Lewes, Falmer.

Parsons, T. (1956). *Family: Socialization and Interaction Processes*. London, Routledge and Kegan Paul.

Parsons, T. (1961). 'The school class as a social system' in A.H. Halsey, *et al.* (eds) *Education, Economy and Society*. New York, The Free Press.

Parsons, T. (1973). 'Youth in the context of American society' in H. Silverstein, (ed.) *The Sociology of Youth: Evolution and Revolution*. New York, Macmillan.

Parsons, T. and Bales, R.F. (1956). *Family: Socialization and Interaction Process*. London, Routledge and Kegan Paul.

Pascall, G. (1986). *Social Policy: A Feminist Analysis*. London, Tavistock.

Pateman, C. (1989). *The Disorder of Women*. Cambridge, Polity/Basil Blackwell.

Payne, J. (1987). 'Does unemployment run in families?' *Sociology*, 2, 199–214.

Payne, J. (1989). 'Unemployment and family formation among young men' *Sociology*, 23(2), 171–91.

Peelo, M. *et al.* (1989). *Surviving Poverty: Probation Work and Benefits Policy*. Wakefield, Yorks, Association of Chief Officers of Probation.

Peelo, M. *et al.* (1990). 'A sense of grievance. Homelessness, poverty and youth offenders' *Youth Social Work*, 2, 12–13.

Phoenix, A. (1991). *Young Mothers?* Cambridge, Polity Press.

Piachaud, D. (1982). 'Patterns of income and expenditure within families' *Journal of Social Policy*, 2(4), 469–82.

Poster, M. (1980). *Critical Theory of the Family*. London, Pluto Press.

Presdee, M. (1990). 'Creating poverty and creating crime: Australian youth policy in the 1980s' in C. Wallace and M. Cross, (eds) *Youth in Transition*. Basingstoke, Falmer.

Prout, A. (1988). ' "Off school sick": mothers' accounts of school sickness absence' *Sociological Review*, 36(4), 765–89.

Raffe, D. (1987). 'Youth unemployment in the United Kingdom 1979–1984' in P. Brown and D.N. Ashton, (eds) *Education, Unemployment and Labour Markets*. Lewes, Falmer.

Raffe, D. (1988). 'The story so far: research on education, training and the labour market' in D. Raffe, (ed.) *Education and Youth Labour Markets*. Lewes, Falmer.

Raffe, D. (1991a). 'The transition from school to work: context, content and the external labour market' in C. Wallace and M. Cross, (eds) *Youth in Transition*. Basingstoke, Falmer.

Raffe, D. (1991b). 'Concepts and theories in the sociology of education and the labour market in the UK'. Paper presented at UK/USSR Workshop *Longitudinal Strategies in the Study of Youth*. Moscow, Youth Institute.

Randall, G. (1988). *No Way Home: Homeless Young People in London*. London, Centrepoint.

Rees, G. and Rees, T.L. (1982). 'Juvenile unemployment and the state between the wars' in T. Rees and P. Atkinson, (eds) *Youth Unemployment and State Intervention*. London, Routledge and Kegan Paul.

Reuter, E.B. (1937). 'The sociology of adolescence', *American Journal of Sociology*, 43, 414–27.

Rex, J. (1972). 'Power' *New Society*, 5 October.

Rich, A. (1981). *Compulsory Heterosexuality and Lesbian Experience*. Only Woman Press pamphlet.

Riseborough, G. (1991). 'The ethnography of career trajectories: YTS'. Paper presented at the ESRC 16–19 Initiative Workshop, *New Findings*, 8–10 March.

Robbins Report (1963). *Higher Education*. London, Committee on Higher Education. HMSO.

Roberts, K. (1968). 'The entry into employment: an approach towards a general theory' *Sociological Review*, 16(2), 165–84.

Roberts, K. (1981). *Leisure*, 2nd Edn. London, Longman.

Roberts, K. (1983). *Youth and Leisure*. London, Allen and Unwin.

Roberts, K. (1984). *School Leavers and Their Prospects. Youth in the Labour Market in the 1980s*. Milton Keynes, Open University Press.

Roberts, K. and Parsell, G. (1988). 'Opportunity structure and career trajectories from age 16–19'. *ESRC 16-19 Initiative Occasional paper*. London, SSRU, City University.

Roberts, K. and Parsell, G. (1990). 'Young people's routes into UK Labour Markets in the late 1980s'. *ESRC 16–19 Initiative Occasional Paper 27*. London, SSRU, City University.

Roberts, K., Dench, S. and Richardson, (1986). 'Youth rates of pay and employment'. Paper presented at the BSA Annual Conference, Loughborough, March.

Roberts, K., Parsell, G. and Connolly, M. (1989). 'Britain's economic recovery, the new demographic trend and young people's transition into the Labour Market'. *ESRC 16–19 Initiative Occasional Paper 8*. London, SSRU, City University.

Roberts, K., Campbell, R. and Furlong, A. (1991). 'Class and gender divisions among young adults at leisure' in C. Wallace and M. Cross, (eds) *Youth in Transition*. Basingstoke, Falmer.

Roll, J. (1990). *Young People: Growing up in the Welfare State*. Occasional Paper No. 10, London, Family Policy Studies Centre.

Roof (1982). 'Young and homeless', May/June.

Saunders, P. (1986). 'Beyond housing classes: the sociological significance of private property rights in the means of consumption' *International Journal of Urban and Regional Research*, 10(1), 202–25.

Scruton, R. (1986). *Sexual Desire*. London, Weidenfeld and Nicolson.

Seabrook, J. (1982). *Unemployment*. London, Quartet Books.

Sharpe, S. (1987). *Falling for Love: Teenage Mothers Talk*. London, Virago Upstarts.

Siltanen, J. (1986). 'Domestic responsibilities and the structuring of employment' in R. Crompton and M. Mann, (eds) *Gender and Stratification*. Cambridge, Polity Press.

Smith, S.J. (1989). *The Politics of 'Race' and Residence*. Oxford, Polity Press.

Social Trends 18 (1988). London, Central Statistical Office, HMSO.

Social Trends 19 (1989). London, Central Statistical Office, HMSO.

Social Trends 21 (1991). London, Central Statistical Office, HMSO.

Solomos, J. (1988). *Black Youth, Racism and the State. The Politics of Ideology and Policy*. Cambridge, Cambridge University Press.

Stacey, J. (1990). *Brave New Families*. New York, Basic.

Stein, M. and Carey, K. (1986). *Leaving Care*. Oxford, Basil Blackwell.

Stewart, G. and Stewart, J. (1988). 'Targeting youth or how the state obstructs young people's independence' *Youth and Policy*, 25, 19–24.

Summers, Y. (1991). 'Women and citizenship: the insane, the insolvent and the inanimate?' in P. Abbott and C. Wallace, (eds) *Gender, Power and Sexuality*. London, Macmillan.

Super, D.E. (1953). 'A theory of vocational development' *American Psychologist*, 8, 185–90.

Thatcher, M. (1987). Interview with Douglas Keay. *Women's Own*, 31 October.

Toffler, A. (1970). *Future Shock*. New York, Random House.

Townsend, P. (1979). *Poverty in the United Kingdom*. Harmondsworth, Pelican.

Turner, B.S. (1990). 'Outline of a theory of citizenship' *Sociology*, 24(2), 189–217.

Turner, B.S. (1991). 'Further specification of the citizenship concept: a reply to M.L. Harrison' *Sociology*, 25(2), 215–18.

Walby, S. (1989). 'Theorizing patriarchy' *Sociology*, 23(2), 213–34.

Walker, A. (1982). *Unqualified and Underemployed: Handicapped Young People in the Labour Market*. London, Macmillan.

Walker, R. (1988). 'The costs of household formation' in R. Walker and G. Parker, (eds) *Money Matters: Income, Wealth and Financial Welfare*. London, Sage.

Wall, R. (1978). 'The age at leaving home' *Journal of Family History*, 3(2), 181–202.

Wallace, C. (1987a). *For Richer, For Poorer: Growing Up In and Out of Work*. London, Tavistock.

Wallace, C. (1987b). 'Between the family and the state: young people in transition' in *The Social World of the Young Unemployed*. London, Policy Studies Institute.

Wallace, C. (1988). 'Between the family and the state' *Youth and Policy*, 25, 35–36.

Wallace, C. (1991a). 'Young people in rural south-west England' *Youth and Policy*, 33, 10–17.

Wallace, C. (1991b). 'Young people and youth policies in Germany' *Youth and Policy*, 32, 20–29.

Wallace, C. (1991c). 'Young people, youth policies and family coping strategies in Britain'. *Mitteilungen des Instituts fuer Wissenschaft und Kunst*, 1, 42–47.

Wallace, C. and Cross, M. (eds) (1990) *Youth in Transition: The Sociology of Youth and Youth Policy*. Basingstoke, Falmer.

Wallace, C., Dunkerley, D. and Cheal, B. (1990). 'The division of labour in farming families'. Working paper, University of Lancaster.

Wallace, C., Dunkerley, D. and Cheal, B. (1991a). 'Post-16 transitions in a rural labour market'. Mimeo, Polytechnic South West.

Wallace, C. *et al.* (1991b). 'Supply and demand in a rural labour market'. Working paper, University of Lancaster.

Warde, A. (1990). 'Introduction to the sociology of consumption' *Sociology*, 24(1), 1–4.

Weber, M. (1961). *General Economic History*, (trans. F. Knight). New York, Collier Books.

White, R. (1990). *No Space of their Own: Young People and Social Control in Australia*. Cambridge, Cambridge University Press.

Wicks, M. (1991). 'Social politics 1979–1992: families, work and welfare'. Paper presented at Social Policy Association Annual Conference, Nottingham, July.

Williams, F. (1989). *Social Policy. A Critical Introduction*. Oxford, Polity.

Willis, P. (1977). *Learning to Labour*. Farnborough, Saxon House.

Willis, P. (1984). 'Youth unemployment' *New Society*, 29 March, 5 April and 12 April.

Wilson, B.R. (1970). *The Youth Culture and the Universities*. London, Faber.

Wilson, P. and Pahl, R. (1988). 'The changing sociological construction of the family' *Sociological Review*, 36(2), 233–72.

Wrench, J., Cross, M. and Barrett, S. (1989). 'Ethnic minorities and the careers service: an assessment of placements'. Department of Employment.

Young, C.M. (1984). 'Leaving home and returning home: a demographic study of young adults in Australia'. *Australian Family Research Conference Proceedings*, Canberra, Vol. 1. Family Formation, Structure, Values, pp. 53–76.

Young, C.M. (1987). *Young People Leaving Home in Australia: The Trend Towards Independence*. Monograph 9. Canberra, Australian Family Formation Project.

Zinnekar, J. (1981). 'Jugend '81: Portrait einer Generation' in Jugenwerk der Deutscher *Shell* (ed.), Jugend '81, Bd. 1, Hamburg, pp. 80–114.

Zweig, F. (1963). *The Student in the Age of Anxiety*. London, Heinemann.

INDEX